GABRIEL MARCEL

BY

SEYMOUR CAIN

REGNERY/GATEWAY, INC.
South Bend, Indiana

This edition published 1979
by Regnery/Gateway, Inc., Book Publishers,
120 West LaSalle Street, South Bend, Indiana 46601
by arrangement with the author.

Library of Congress Catalog Card Number: 79-50156
International Standard Book Number: 0-89526-905-8
Manufactured in the United States of America

CONTENTS

REFERENCES

I have used my own translations in the citations from Marcel's works, indicating the location of each passage in the original text and also (in parentheses) in the published English translation whenever there is one. In the text I have given the titles in English; in the footnotes I have listed the original French titles. I have omitted bibliographical information from the footnotes where it is given in the bibliography at the end of this book.

S. C.

PREFACE TO THE GATEWAY EDITION

This new preface to a work whose foundations were laid over a quarter of a century ago is written with both joy and regret. The satisfaction derives from the assurance that the subject is still considered important and that this presentation of it is still deemed worthy of being republished and reread. The sadness derives from the fact that the very living thinker who is described appreciatively in the original preface is no longer with us in the flesh. Moreover, for me personally, there is the sense of loss (perhaps illusory) of what seems to have been a greater, more open, more creative time—the time in which this little work was made.

Since this work was first published, there have been some heartening developments in human studies. Paul Ricoeur's monumental work in hermeneutical theory, for instance, has deepened the cultural world's grasp of spiritual meaning. (Ricoeur, it should be noted, was a one-time disciple and a long-time friend and colleague of Marcel's.) Also there is the magnificent work of Mircea Eliade in the history and phenomenology of religions, recuperating the deepest strata of man's spiritual patrimony, a work that has come to full fruition and recognition during the interim. These and similar endeavors by other inquirers would seem to have opened the way to a renewed, expanded appreciation of Marcel.

Yet for the contemporary academic mind (which tends to set its imprint on the wider cultural mind) there seems to be a deep-set inhibition against following Marcel along his tentative, unprogrammatic, winding way. We need not delude ourselves. Academics and attendant intellectuals want treatises, systems, operational codes and apparatuses, for tangible enterprises and gains in the cultural marketplace; or, if not that, at least portentous pronouncements on great big ontological subject matters, whereby at least to impress themselves of their own importance and *raison d'être*. Also of legal tender in that marketplace are, of course, the ephemeral 90-week wonders of the dead God, play cult, secular religion, and other marvelous meanderings that are ritually rechewed and regurgitated by hard-up religious journalism every ten years or so.

Unfortunately, or, rather, fortunately, Gabriel Marcel does not belong in that company. He is hardly the type of philosopher who would deplane at an airport and immediately announce to avid reporters, armed with note-pads and flash cameras: "Ladies and gentlemen, God is dead!" Such a grim pronouncement, he has noted, if it must come, has to be done in fear and trembling, in private anguish, not in the glare of spotlights. Marcel's appeal is no more to the image-world of media publicity than it is to the ponderous-grave realm of academic treatises. What he has to communicate comes across only to a quiet, open ungrasping attention.

In our last meeting in Paris, a few months before his death, Marcel, aging, ailing, and growing blind, was still the marvelous conversationalist, witty, full of good humor, interested in everything, joy percolating throughout. Yet this veteran metaphysician and phenomenologist of hope expressed gloomy forebodings about the immediate future of Western society and culture, which he saw as

6

increasingly dominated by mechanical techniques, spiritually polluted and asphyxiated, bowed down by the daily dross of vulgarized mass culture. He was convinced that things were bound to get a good deal worse before they got any better—but he did hope for a coming transformation.

As I said in my memorial tribute to Marcel, "It was not that he had given up all hope, any more than he had given up faith or love. He simply insisted on looking candidly at the concrete present situation, out of which any salutary transformation must come. And in his personal career and stance he presented us with an encouraging example of the humanness and spiritual openness that are still attainable in the present age." ("Gabriel Marcel (1889–1973): An Example of Humanness," *The Christian Century*, October 31, 1973.)

I have decided to let this early effort stand as it is, warts and all. I do not believe it a good idea to look over one's shoulder *ex post facto* and revise the expression of an earlier decade through older, and perhaps wiser, eyes. Certainly I would not be so polemically dismissive of analytical and linguistic philosophy today. For one thing, since then, I have fallen, for a time, under the spell of Wittgenstein. For another, I have realized that the newer, largely Anglo-American schools of thought, as any significant school of philosophy, have made their contribution to our collective intellectual and cultural endeavors, and that we must be docile enough, in the original sense, to learn what is valuable in what they have to teach. Also, these schools have become subtler and deeper, and much less dismissive themselves.

In addition, I feel a bit sheepish about at least

one inelegancy in my translation of key Marcellian terms: *disponsibilité* and *indisponsibilité*. They are better translated "availability" and "unavailability," not "disposability" and "indisposability," as I usually have it here. The literal translation is not quite right; it is "insufficiently domesticated," as an acute reviewer for the *Times Literary Supplement* noted at the time. *Peccavi*. Please note and correct it as you go along.

CHICAGO, September, 1978.

PREFACE

This book is an introduction to the thought of Gabriel Marcel. It deals with his basic philosophical tendencies and concerns as they are revealed in his writings, while giving little attention to Marcel's connections with his predecessors and contemporaries. This concentration has been motivated by the particular requirements of a short introductory essay. Besides, other hands have assembled portmanteau volumes that point out the similarities and differences between present day existential and phenomenological thinkers.

It is over a decade since I began the study of Marcel's writings. In the middle 1950's I wrote a detailed, scholarly work on Marcel's thought, upon which this book is based. At that time Mr. Marcel generously extended his aid by answering my many and probably sometimes vexing inquiries. I also met him in Canada in 1956 and in the United States in 1961, and encountered a warmth and geniality which I am afraid I have not conveyed in this philosophical study. Marcel's gaiety and charm set him off from the stereotype of the solemn philosopher. Those philosophical commentators who call longingly for a "laughing philosopher" in our time might do well to seek him in the Rue de Tournon in Paris. Marcel, with his wit and bubbling good humour and *joie de vivre*, has been with us for a long time. These qualities of his, however, are difficult to convey in a study of thought.

I am indebted to Dr. V. J. McGill, Mr. Peter Wolff, and Mr. Gerald Temaner for their comments on the various chapters as they were being

9

written and to my wife, Betty Jean, for her constant editorial aid, criticisms, and suggestions. That this book appears at all is originally due to my late master, colleague, and friend, Joachim Wach, who first urged and persuaded me to do a study of Marcel's thought. To him, who is always with me, I dedicate this work.

San Francisco, January, 1962.

I

Marcel's Way

Gabriel Marcel has doggedly and courageously followed his own way throughout a philosophical career that covers half a century. An existential philosopher decades before the term "existential" became fashionable, a phenomenological thinker long before phenomenology became a central concern of European philosophy, a religious thinker at a time when religion had not yet regained respectability in philosophical circles—Gabriel Marcel has been a herald of our times.

Marcel belongs in the illustrious company of Martin Buber, Nicolas Berdyaev, and others who have struggled to renew and reintegrate the shattered human spirit in this terrible century. Like Buber and Berdyaev, he has held fast to his unique personal vision, while at the same time speaking as a member of an historical religious community. In his case this may have been doubly hard, since he had to take the path of formal conversion.

Marcel's conversion to Catholicism in his fortieth year was the culmination of years of patient metaphysical inquiry and fulfilled an exigent personal quest. Since his conversion, he has continued to explore his major metaphysical and "metapsychical" concerns, without feeling bound to conform to any finished philosophical system or prescribed habits of thought. Gabriel Marcel is a nonconformist Catholic philosopher—non-Thomistic and even anti-Thomistic. He is a leading existential philosopher—associated in histories of contemporary thought with Martin Heidegger and Jean-Paul Sartre—who proclaims a human community centred in God. He is French to the core, a disciple of Henri Bergson, and at the same time a debtor to German and British idealists, as well as to two American philosophers—Josiah Royce and William E. Hocking.[1]

Readers both in Europe and America have sensed something inimitable and precious in the writings of Marcel. He does not fit the usual picture of the philosopher—we associate no university chair, nor philosophical system, nor ponderous treatise with his name. Yet in his own way, speaking in his own tone, he communicates to us the perennial philosophical quest for contact with reality.

Marcel is not the kind of thinker who has a system of cubbyholes—crude or intricate—into which he puts all the stuff of his life and thought, and, when this fails, throws what will not fit into the waste-basket of intellectual oblivion. He is not the kind of thinker for whom things must come out even, with no overlaps or disjointedness, with everything formulable in logically consistent and meaningful statements. He is not the kind of thinker for whom the world is a neat pyramid of billiard balls, in hierarchical gradation, from the electron-flash to the Absolute—neat, clean, and well-lighted, with everything in its place. He is not the kind of thinker who advances with deliberate and systematic method along a route that has been carefully mapped beforehand to reach points where definite answers will meet definite questions. He is not the

[1] See Appendix.

12

kind of thinker who presents his thought in a 1–2–3 order, following an objective outline.

Marcel's way has been different. It has been more like that of the writer or artist who says or makes what demands to be said or made by him, in response to an urgent inner demand; a demand, however, which cannot be fulfilled by his conscious will alone, according to plan and schedule, for there can be no image of its fulfillment before the creative act, which is his whole life-work. The Book the creative writer writes is the body of all his writings, sounding all the themes he has been concerned with. But he does not know what the Book will say until he has written it, and even then he cannot sum it up in a formula.

Thus Marcel has groped and striven along the labyrinthine ways that took him from the desert world of nineteenth century idealist philosophy to the rich fruitlands of life in its unique and individual reality—and to a "concrete philosophy". The first part of his early work, the *Metaphysical Journal*, which traces the beginning of his journey, is painfully arid and transcendental, as Marcel himself later acknowledged. The evocative analyses of human existence and the "concrete philosophy" of his later days are not conclusions that follow inevitably from his early thought or that could have been deduced beforehand.

Marcel did not keep this philosophical diary to himself as a private work-book—as he had originally intended—but presented it to the public as a philosophical work in itself. His motivations for doing this were not merely a dogged honesty in presenting the living day-to-day record of meditations that grope and make false starts and double back on themselves. Empirical scientists could do and have done the same thing to record the actual processes of inquiry. But Marcel was doing something more: he was saying that this is what philosophical thought is really like, and that an expository treatise, with the sober schoolman's beginning-middle-and-end, neatly sectioned and numbered, gives a distorted and flattened picture of what such thought really is. The "way" and the "what" of Marcel's thought are bound together—indeed, the way is the what.

Marcel has retained a preference for the diary mode of presentation and returned to it on more than one occasion. Another favourite mode is the phenomenological essay, where Marcel takes the reader with him on a search for the meaning of specific human realities and concerns, such as hope, fidelity, "I" and "Thou". He calls on the reader to participate with him in an intuitive groping for meaning and to respond to the many evocations the phenomenon calls forth, so that he may gain insight into the meanings intended by our elemental speech. This is not a matter of following an argument, of assenting to or dissenting from certain statements, of logical analysis and understanding. The "understanding" Marcel calls for is more like the appreciation and insight called for in our encounter with art, history, and religion, and in our meetings with other persons.

Marcel's philosophical stance is essentially auditory, rather than optical. He is not the spectator who looks for a world of structures that may be clearly and distinctly seen. He listens to and responds to "voices" and "calls" that make up the symphony of being, which for him is ultimately a supra-rational unity beyond images, words, and concepts. From an early age, long before he knew who he was and where he was going, music furnished him with the concrete embodiment of that realm which can only be heard and not seen, can only be participated in but not demonstrated. It also furnished him with the paradigmatic form of expression to which his philosophy tried to approximate. For in music the way and the what are indubitably inseparable. Music does not provide us with an idea-content that we may abstract and consider apart from our listening, our actual participation in the music, our meeting with it, being with it. Music does not furnish us with objects to look at or grasp, nor is it the effluvia of an interior monologue.

Music has played a key role in Marcel's thought, continually presenting him with a level of reality and a mode of relation that transcend the limits of idealist and empiricist philosophies. He attributes to it—especially to Bach's music—his understanding of religious experience and his own religious development. In Marcel's own musical creation improvisation has been his favourite mode. This emphasis on the immediate and spontaneous mode undoubtedly reveals something characteristic about Marcel's spirit. It also indicates that the participation which he considers essential in our experience of music is not merely a matter of listening to or playing the music other people have written. The most spontaneous form of musical composition is also a participation in and a response to a reality "outside" us. Improvisation is not merely "self-expression", the external manifestation of subjective feelings and impressions—it is *dialogue*.

An unsympathetic interpreter might be tempted to see in this emphasis on music and the realm of supra-rational harmony a typical romantic flight from the everyday realm of suffering and fault, of strife and cross purposes, of doubt and despair. But long before Marcel devoted himself to these very topics in his later philosophical writings, he had dealt with human conflict and confusion through his third form of expression—dramatic writing. He tells us in his personal *mémoire* that he was very early confronted with the fact of irreconcilable and incompatible personalities in his own family circle and that desolation and despair were his earliest companions. It was these incompatibilities and these negative aspects that he dealt with in his plays, the first of which he published in 1914, at the time of his earliest metaphysical journals. Again it is illuminating to note that the literary mode he found most natural was not narration or description, but drama—not statements about, but presentations of the human situation through characters, that is, through "voices". For Marcel, always the auditor, thought of his plays not as "spectacles", but as "symphonies", in which the characters sound various parts in the whole—which is meant to be *heard* even more than to be seen.

This, then, was the second model for his thought: dramatic enactment, a form in which whatever is to be communicated is expressed through the interactions of individual characters, each of whom is unique and unpredictable and yet contributes to the action of the whole. The "irreducible originality" and "singularity of perspective" of action were important concepts for a thinker who rejected the notion that concrete realities can be reduced to formulas. Quite early he opposed the absolute idealist notion that concrete realities can be integrated (thought) into the great All or One, and rejected the idea that an intelligible whole, a *summa* of reality, is possible. He held to the decisively new-making (or new-breaking) quality of action, whereby action makes a real difference that cannot be thought away and integrated into some abstract whole. In action he found a concrete and dramatic relation between realities, for to act is "to take up a position" against something or someone, the "other" (partner or opponent) in a dramatic whole. Abstract thought attempts to do away with this essential over-againstness, the twoness involved when a real self confronts a real "other" in action.

Marcel chose drama because he had to "make it new", and, above all, to make thought concrete, to body it forth. He chose tragedy, a tragedy of thought, of conscience in tension. In his dramatic creation he concretely opposed the idealism, rationalism, and positivism he was to defy in his philosophical works. "I am convinced," he says, "that it is in drama and through drama that metaphysical thought grasps and defines itself *in concreto*."[1]

Thus in Marcel's life-work there are three paths: first, the way of music, of spontaneous improvisation, pointing to a realm where communion is fully achieved; second, the way of metaphysical meditation and phenomenological analysis, locating in thought the beacons and reefs on man's spiritual journey; and third, the way of dramatic presentation, acting out in concrete characters and situations what is explored independently in the metaphysical meditations. To follow Marcel on

---

[1] *Positions et approches concrètes du mystère ontologique*, p. 67 (English trans. in *The Philosophy of Existence*, p. 15). Hereafter cited as *Mystère ontologique*.

his way, we need not necessarily accompany him on all of the three paths. The first is closed to those who do not have his musical predisposition and do not share his gift for improvisation; and, in the nature of the case, we cannot even have "documents" of his improvisation; furthermore, his written compositions are scanty and not his major creative contribution. The second way is fully documented—in his metaphysical journals, in the phenomenological essays to be found in *Homo Viator, Being and Having, The Mystery of Being, From Refusal to Invocation*, and in many periodical essays. The third way is also open to us, for about two dozen volumes of Marcel's plays exist in French. (As yet few of them are translated into English.) It is significant that the essay summing up Marcel's mature thought ("On the Ontological Mystery") first appeared as the epilogue to one of his plays.

The general reader of philosophy may be annoyed at having to follow a man's thought through a disconnected series of diary entries, essays, and plays. He usually expects books with a single topic, stating a definite problem, and proceeding through a series of chapters, more or less systematically arranged. He likes to have a stable and definite object clearly and directly presented for his consideration. Marcel's philosophical works do not satisfy this expectation. Those that are not journals are collections of essays, held together by a keynote title and a pervasive set of concerns. The one exception perhaps is his series of Gifford Lectures on *The Mystery of Being*, given late in his career, a belated attempt at a quasi-systematic presentation of his thought. Even in this work, however, Marcel refuses to impose an external, objective unity on his thought and to translate the original tone and colour into some bland didactic presentation. Again he follows the way of evocation, allusion, and suggestion, which is typical of his other works.

Thus the reader may have to overcome some initial annoyance at Marcel's unconventional mode of presentation, but he will then find himself in contact with something far richer, deeper, and humanly truer than ordinary didactic treatises in philosophy. Marcel does not force, he does not dazzle, he does not proceed from a cut-off intellectual part of himself. He does not force us into procrustean definitions and postulates, and proceed with logical rigour to a forced set of conclusions. He calls, he listens, and invites us to listen with him, as he starts off from a theme and follows it patiently and openly, with a delicate and intricate form of concrete analysis, which concludes not with a Q.E.D. through a necessary sequence of propositions, but with a fulness of discerned meanings through immersion in a reality which must be felt and heard, rather than conceived and seen.

Let us in this little book listen to the sounds of his major themes.

II

The Sand Castle and the World

Marcel, like many modern philosophers, worked out his thought in a struggle against idealist philosophy. This struggle has usually been intramural, a civil war within the mind; from Kierkegaard to Sartre, those who have risen up against idealism have done so from within idealism. Marcel, as his early journals indicate, is a good example of this revolt from within.

He was predisposed to idealist thought, having an abhorrence of the empirical world as brutish, chaotic, and impure, an impulse toward a transcendental realm beyond life, and a rare capacity for abstract thought and metaphysical meditation. Yet there were also many forces within him working against the notion of a universally legislating human mind at the centre of the universe. He refused to deny the reality that he was and the reality he experienced. He refused to admit that he was essentially mind or abstract thought and that the outer world was merely his mental construction. There was a real world of real beings outside his mind, to which he belonged and with which he had real relations that were not merely mental. His body was real and his sensations were real, and they were not to be explained away. And experience, properly understood, was something deeper and higher and fuller than abstract thought—not merely raw material to be transcended and worked up: it was a goal to be attained rather than a starting-point to get away from.

As Marcel saw it, any question as to the reality of the external world, as against the indubitable reality of the thinking self, is ridiculous, and the traditional distinction between appearance and reality—between the world of experience and a metaphysical realm—is misleading. Hence his religious search, recorded in the early journals, for the reality which underlies our experience—an experience which includes both sensation and religious faith. Here he sounds already the themes of sensation, body, and faith which he was to develop more fully later. He deals with them here as an academic and abstract problem, as part of his attempt to demonstrate that there are aspects of human experience that are unverifiable by objective thought. This was a riposte not only against idealist philosophy but also against empirical psychology. He was searching, in the grandiloquent jargon of the day, for the "transcendental conditions of faith in its purity".

This formal approach was in keeping with the religious vacuum of his boyhood and youth, which he reveals in his personal *mémoire*.[1] Brought up by a sceptical, pagan father who did not even bother to have him baptized and by an aunt who put her faith in ethical culture and rigorous will, he was completely without religious training or knowledge in the traditional sense. Without either personal repugnance to or desire for religious faith, he approached it as something that existed and was to be taken seriously on its own grounds,

---

[1] "Regard en arrière", in *Existentialisme chrétien*, by Etienne Gilson, *et al.* Translated as "An Essay in Autobiography", in *The Philosophy of Existence*.

not to be explained away. At this time he passed no judgement on its metaphysical reality and validity, but simply confined himself to demonstrating that such a judgement could not be made from a position outside faith.

It would be facile to suggest that Marcel reflected himself out of reflection or came to faith through reflection. We should remember, however, the three-fold expression of Marcel's spirit and see these reflections as the working out in thought of what is developed otherwise in his plays and music. Marcel's first plays—*Grace* and *The Sand Castle*, published in 1914 under the common title of *The Invisible Threshold*—show a perceptive and serious concern for religious themes. The minor character Olivier in *Grace* may express in some measure the concerns of the young Marcel—an unbeliever who is waiting on grace, envious of other people's faith, struggling for what he loves and reveres despite a harmful sceptical education. It is he who proclaims the reality of faith at the close of the play, though still in idealist terms.

After the writing of these plays and of the First Part of the *Metaphysical Journal* came Marcel's decisive experiences during the First World War. This was the time of what we may term his first "conversion", the importance of which he fully realized later in life. Barred by delicate health from active war service, Marcel worked for the French Red Cross, dealing with the "missing" and the relatives anxious for knowledge of them. Somehow the "missing" lost for him the abstract quality of mere names, ranks, and serial numbers, and became real beings, addressing a personal appeal to him, to which he responded with interest and anguish. This open sensitivity revealed to him realities which are ignored by objective history and social research.

Next in the personal influences on the development of his thought were the "metapsychical" experiments, which convinced him of the reality of a realm where communication takes place other than by the normal psycho-sensory modes. The Second Part of the *Metaphysical Journal* is full of discussions of telepathy, clairvoyance, necromancy, prophecy, automatic writing, psychometry and other "metapsychical" phenomena. These experiences had a lasting effect on Marcel, and, despite opposition from academic philosophers and from churchmen, he held consistently that an honest philosopher must take this realm into account in his thought at least as a metaphysical possibility, and not dogmatically reject it. No prejudice or pressure ever forced him to withdraw from this position, which he held to be vital in his struggle against idealism.

It might be said that Marcel broke away from idealism through working out his idea of *participation*. This is the basic concept for the entire discussion of existence, sensation, incarnation, knowledge of others, and religious belief in the Second Part of the *Metaphysical Journal*. Whatever the term "participation" may mean in other philosophies, here it does not mean the partaking of the mind in ideas or in an ideal realm, nor does it mean a fusion or identity of the soul with an indeterminate, impersonal absolute. Participation for Marcel is the immediate communion between real, determinate, distinct beings, who yet retain their distinctness and determinateness. It is the elemental experience of being with other beings, not the mental grasp or noetic vision of ideas or essences; the global experience of "we are", not the partial function of "I think". This primal immediacy cannot be observed, grasped, or verified from the outside; it cannot be translated into ideas and images, but only lived and relived, evoked and recalled. The participation between beings is knowable only through participation, through sympathetic mediation and communion. This also applies to the relation between me and my past, for memory is not a matter of sorting out and grasping a collection of old snapshots and souvenirs, but a mode of being with my past, for my past is part of me and when I re-collect myself I am my past. Memory is a matter of communion, of being-with, not of communication, not of a transmission of messages. The same is true of my future, which is "mine" only as I am with it; it has to do with what I *am*, not what I *have*.

Marcel developed this principle of participation in meditations on his "metapsychical" concerns and applied it to clairvoyance, spiritism, psychometry, and prophecy. He also applied it, then and later, to the central religious experiences of prayer, faith, and "trial", as well as to the primary example of sympathetic communion between human beings—the love between a man and a woman. Faith and love are, indeed, the highest and most radiant embodiments of participation in Marcel's world. But he first developed his idea at the more fundamental level of physical existence, with regard to the basic experience we have of our bodies and the sensation we have of other beings. His sensualist metaphysics may seem surprising at first and difficult to reconcile with his metapsychical and religious concerns. Marcel's purpose becomes clearer, however, if we consider what he was trying to reject, to escape from, and what he was trying to arrive at and affirm.

Modern philosophy, from Descartes through the nineteenth century idealists, had made problematic the unity of mind and body and the relation between the self and the world. Common to all the forms of modern idealism is the absolute indubitability and pre-eminent reality of thought, consciousness, or mind. Sensation, in this view, is the raw, inchoate, vague material that is worked into clear and definite thought patterns that explain or interpret the world. Thought is active and constructive; sensation is passive, mere receptivity. The assumption of this intermediary process between sense-experience and cognition raised the question of whether we can really know anything besides our own constructions. Inquirers asked:

(1) whether we have certain knowledge of the physical world, and
(2) whether knowledge of a metaphysical world is possible.

These and similar questions were posited and answered in various ways by the different schools of modern philosophy.

The young Marcel worked his way through the most important eighteenth and nineteenth century idealists, with some of whom, notably Schelling, he felt more affinity than with others. But he felt that at the root of all idealist thought was the basic and vicious error of dissociating mind and body, and thus cutting the mind off from the full integral self and from the world to which the self belongs. Our primary experience, our most ordinary sensations, and even thought itself, Marcel held, become unintelligible on this basis. Hence he regarded materialist and sensualist philosophies as a salutary protest against a disastrous error. But he was satisfied neither with the empiricist or idealist version of sensation nor with the materialist or idealist version of the body. He set out to give his own account of sensation and incarnation, not only to bring forth their true nature, but to show what existence is and how it may be affirmed.

In the first place, as against Descartes, Marcel held that it is _sensation_ that is indubitable, not thought. The early Marcel might have said, "I _feel_, hence I am", for I am my feeling. Sensation, with its infallibility in its immediate unreflected, uninterpreted state is the primal model for religious faith. Sensation is a mode of being; reflection, ideas, and images only distort it and reduce the untranslatable feeling that I _am_ to perceptions that I _have_ and can transmit to others. Feeling is a matter of real conjunction and association, not of merely private impressions and images; it is real power, being, and quality that I meet and that meets me through feeling. This is not merely a matter of the primary and secondary qualities—of shape, and weight, and touch, and colour, and smell—but of the quality or tone of the room I sleep in at night, the intangible "charm" of a person, the quality of a "scene" or of the whole "ambiance" of a particular place and moment. Real power or being appears to me as felt quality; for instance, the basic "feel smell" of a flower appears to me as colour or perfume, and there is a temporary coalescence of sensation and sensum.

None of this happens merely passively, without enlisting my intent and interest, as do subliminal perceptions or Humian impressions. "To feel is

26

not to receive but to participate immediately."[1] Or rather, it is to receive, as I receive a guest. I must open the door and let him in and grasp his hand and give myself. Without this "hospitality", to use Marcel's later term, there is no real reception, and so with feeling and with all the acts that reproduce it, such as memory. The lack of this requisite openness and giving, of sympathetic participation, may explain why some philosophers denigrate feeling as something crude, vague, or frivolous—to be transcended in pure thought, metaphysical universals, or rational systems—and provide so inadequate an account of human experience.

Similarly, "my body"—not body, a body, or the body, but *my* body—is indubitably existent, indeed, the type for all existence, the basis for all feeling of and attending to the world, and hence of all thought and dialectic. This is not merely a material or biological truism, in the sense that the body is functionally intermediary between the mind and the world. Prior to and more basic than this "instrumental" mediation of the body, Marcel discerns a basic sense of my body, a primal immediate feeling of myself for my body, which is the basis of the "sympathetic" mediation of my body for other beings. This immediate participation of myself in my body is the model for my participation in things, for my relation to the world and for the existence I assert of things. As I participate in my body, it participates in things, and I belong to the world through my body. It is the centre of my universe. My awareness and affirmation of my body precedes all my awareness and affirmation of existence. When I say that something exists, I

[1] *Journal métaphysique*, p. 251 (English trans., p. 258).

27

mean, "This being or thing is of the same nature as my body and belongs to the same world", which is bound to me by the same "thread" of immediate participation that binds me to my body.[1]

It is here that Marcel breaks with the whole subject-object mode of affirming existence. He opposes *existence* to *objectivity*. Existence is sensible and immediately participated in through sensation. It is not an object of thought or consciousness of the thinking self, the *cogito*. It is beneath or beyond dialectic—beyond verification or demonstration by rational argument. Existence, like sensation and body, is indubitable, not hypothetical. In a journal entry in February 1922, Marcel notes:

I tend to dissociate radically the ideas of existence and objectivity; and it is perhaps especially from this viewpoint that my previous reflections on the body are important. Things exist for me insofar as I regard them as prolongations of my body. But, on the other hand, I think of them as objects only insofar as I place myself at the viewpoint of "others", of "anybody" (*n'importe qui*), and finally of "nobody". If I now claim to eliminate from this objective world all that "comes from me", (and the expression is as equivocal as possible), in the last analysis there remains nothing but a web of abstractions, to which, by a singular illusion, I persist in attributing that existence, which, I repeat, is *exclusive* of pure objectivity.[2]

Thus things exist for me not through objective thought, but through the same immediate participation whereby my body is present to me.

[1] *Journal métaphysique*, p. 305 (English trans., p. 315).
[2] *Ibid.*, p. 273 (English trans., p. 281).

Existence cannot be reduced to objectivity. What exists for me is not a detached object for spectatorial thought, but something with which I am actually involved and which "takes account" of me as I take account of it. Real mutuality and intercourse take place. Existence is co-existence, and being is being-with. When I assert the existence of anything I affirm the same self-being that I affirm of my body—the existence-type for all things. I do not put myself at a distance from it, assume the disinterested, unloving, ungiving attitude of the detached observer, and mirror it on the lens of my consciousness for analytical discrimination and definition.

Existence is not something to grasp and arrange and tot up in my mental balance-book. Existence is *worth-ful*, and the more intensely and fully we open ourselves to existence the more valuable is our own existence. The affirmation of existence is an expression of vitality and generosity. "Cry *is!*": that is in effect what Marcel urges as he ends the tortuous windings of his *Metaphysical Journal* on a lyrical note which leads from metaphysics to ethics. He links the sense of "presence"—and presence is always "sensible"—to the value of existence, and warns that "we are worth proportionately less as our affirmation of existence is more restricted, more pallid, more hesitant".[1] To cry "Is" is to say "Yes". And, as his discussion of religious experience emphasizes, to say "Yes" is to say "Thou".

Marcel summed up his meditations on sensation, incarnation, and existence in the paper "Existence and Objectivity", first published in 1925 and later appended to the *Metaphysical Journal*. This essay

[1] *Journal métaphysique*, p. 306 (English trans., p. 317).

is of the first importance for anyone who wants to understand Marcel's thought. As a succinct expression of his early thought, it belongs with his later essays on "Ontological Mystery", and "Concrete Philosophy". According to Lalande's standard French philosophical dictionary, the 1925 essay is the first public use of the term "existence" and "existential" by a French thinker in the Kierkegaardian, present-day sense.[1]

The views expressed in "Existence and Objectivity" will be familiar enough to those who have read carefully the journal entries on feeling, "my body", and existence. The paper contains, however, a fuller delineation of what Marcel means by the term "existence" and at times a more lyrical and dramatic expression of the problems discussed. He speaks of the "insularity" which objective thought wrongfully tries to establish between subject and object, and hails the "integral human experience grasped in its trembling and tragic life", which systematic rationalism mutilates or ignores. He presents the problem of the affirmation or doubt of existence as an either/or decision, made necessary by the weakening of our primary sense of existence by idealistic thought. Against the arbitrary decree of absolute scepticism he chooses the opposite decree of absolute affirmation—that existence is indubitable. But this is not mere arbitrariness, Marcel insists, for to recognize the primacy of existence as against the imperious claims of mind requires "real spiritual humility". I recognize over against myself "effective" and "absolute" presence.

This is an affirmation that is both "global"

[1] André Lalande, *Vocabulaire technique et critique de la philosophie* (Paris: Presses universitaires de France, 1947), p. 308.

and concrete. It is not the attribution of existence to a finite something, as its predicate; nor is it the assertion of some abstract Existence-in-general dissociable from individual existents. Existents and existence are indissociable. We cannot speak of one apart from the other. Existence cannot be thought, nor can it be determined by some table of abstract characteristics or differentia, nor arrived at by hypotheses of the "if . . . then" variety. We affirm existence through immediate knowledge and participation in the order of feeling, where what affirms and what is affirmed become one, each being "global" and confused—and not precise, objective affirmations. All that we can do by thought is to *recognize* the existence that has become present through immediate participation; we are unable to *establish* existence through abstract reflection. The latter attempt makes reality unintelligible, alienates the self from the world, and leads to doubt about the existence of the self, to the philosophical nightmares of the last three centuries which haunt both our days and our nights. This essay, written a generation ago, is Marcel's early attempt to describe the nightmare of alienation and provide a few hints as to where the way might lie toward integral wholeness and a real world.

That is why Marcel fights here against the instrumentalist view of the body and the idealist view of the self. *My* body is not simply an instrument for receiving and sending messages, and sensation cannot be explained in these terms. This mechanical view is applicable only when *I* am not involved, where it is a matter of relations between things that I view spectatorially. But *my* body is something I *am*, not that I *use*, and I cannot take myself out of the picture through some dubious "ideal disincarnation". My body is not my tool and it is inseparable from me, just as I am essentially incarnate and inseparable from it. I am my body/self, in a world of other body/selves—not of ideas. It is other body/selves that are present to me through feeling, not physical "messages" transmitted through the body and translated into thought by my mind. My body is not an intermediary term between my self and the world, because it cannot be made into an objective term apart from me. This "intellectually indefectible bond" between my self and my body must also—by extrapolation or analogy—characterize other body/selves. I must grasp them "globally", through sympathetic participation, as integral body/selves, not analytically as minds in bodies to which they are somehow related. Anything else is nonsense, perversity, and alienation, and leaves me lost and alone in a dark and tangled wood of philosophical paradoxes, cut off from myself and other beings. Such alienation leaves me on the one hand with a "mannequin-reality", a bare substance dressed up in appearances by the thinking self; on the other with an "animated notice", a fictional personage, upon whose relations to my body (detached from the real me) I vainly try to reflect. And, of course, I treat other persons, other minds as "mental effigies" unrelated to their bodies. I reduce everything to ideas.

Marcel's metaphysics in this early piece is not only sensualist and incarnational; it is also activist. He points to the body/self union as a "metaphysical form of haecceity . . . an indivisible which reflection cannot get at".[1] He also points to the

---

[1] *Journal métaphysique*, p. 328 (English trans., p. 338).

unity of idea/act/person, as in the example of lifting my arm. *In the situation*, they are indivisible, and "there is no science possible of the transition from the idea to the act", which is misrepresented as a "communication between distinct spheres".[1] *When I act*, I destroy the fiction of "ideal disincarnation" and regain the body/self unity that is broken by analysis into a duality of instrumentalist and instrument. Marcel rejects all the dualisms—that of subject and object, mind and body, senser and sensum, idea and act, thought and existence—for the unities of global existence, "my body", sensible presence, and personal action.

Marcel admits that systematic knowledge, objective analysis, and the instrumentalist view of the body have their place and serve a useful scientific purpose. He sees even in scientific inquiry a hidden "dialectic", or dialogue, between the searcher and the object of his inquiries.[2] But he insists that this type of thought is utterly inadequate for grasping the full reality of the self and its relation to the world. Only abstract partial functions are thus grasped, and if this approach monopolizes our thought and attitude, we are left with the alienation and emptiness alluded to above, and with the dubious consolation and amusement of a host of paradoxes and problems to make sense of. Hence the need for what he later called "secondary reflection" which makes whole what analytical thought has imprudently put asunder, a reintegration and reincarnation that "consciously re-establishes the state of indivision which an elementary reflection has broken".[3] We are saved

---

[1] *Journal métaphysique*, p. 329 (English trans., p. 339).
[2] *Ibid.*, p. 316 (English trans., p. 326).
[3] *Ibid.*, pp. 321, 326 (English trans., pp. 331, 336).

from the mutilations and distortions of reflection by a deeper reflection. And hence the return to what his critics call an "obsolete ontology", for we hunger for "a universe that is not a world of ideas".[1] Only in a real world can our minds find root and our experience be rendered intelligible. And only in such a world can prayers bear fruit, not in the "sandcastle" of idealist thought.

[1] *Journal métaphysique,* p. 321 f. (English trans., p. 331).

III

Thou

Participation is the central idea of Marcel's *Meta-physical Journal*. The *I–thou* relation is the most important development of this central idea and is basic to his theory of religious experience. "All relation of being to being is personal . . .", he says; ". . . all spiritual life is essentially a dialogue . . .", and again: "The dyadic relation is what in my previous inquiries I called participation".[1] This dialogical turning toward another being as *thou* is entirely different from the dialectical posture toward otherness as *it*, just as address-and-response ("invocation") is distinct from question-and-answer ("information"). The dialogical relation is mutual, and involves a withness and what Marcel calls a "finality"—a particular address or intention—that is excluded in the dialectical relation.

When I think something or someone as *it* or *he* or *they*, I make detached, objective judgements in which the other figures as the object of my thought —passive, supine, and not affecting me. I seek accurate, discriminating knowledge about it. I handle it in my mind—via terms, concepts, and judgements—but it has essentially nothing to do with me. It has an independent existence and attributes apart from me and my thought of it. On the other hand, when I think or address other

[1] *Journal métaphysique*, pp. 137, 155 (English trans., 137, 155 f.).

35

beings as *thou*, I am wholly involved and affected in a relation that requires the withness and response of the other. Here the other is not the object of my thought, or admitted only as an item in my mind, but is my partner in being—real "twoness" is necessarily present here. And only as the other is truly *thou* for me, do I truly become *I* for myself, for the *thou* discovers me to myself. I am truly *I* only over against a *thou* for whom I also am a *thou*.

Another significant aspect of the *I–thou* relation is that it involves undefined and unspecified realities on both sides. It is not the relation of a particular, definite, characterized someone (*un tel*) to another such someone or something. On the contrary, the "global" wholeness of the *I* is directed toward ("intends") the unlimited, unspecified being of the *thou*. The *I* does not love the other because he has certain good qualities, or because the *I* has judged the other to possess specific intellectual, moral, and religious virtues. He simply affirms the other, says "Yes", to him. In love, says Marcel, we refuse to treat the beloved being as a construable, explicable, predictable, expressible "content" that may be conceived in common categories. "For the lover, love is logically anterior to all possible reduction."[1] In an accidental meeting between strangers on a train, for example, there is a transition from the exchange of information—personal "data" and opinions—to a real withness of being, from the "triadic" discussion about *it*-items to a dialogue within a *we*-unity in which each becomes a being for himself as he becomes a being for the other.[2] Of course, this dialogue need not

[1] *Journal métaphysique*, p. 228 (English trans., p. 234).
[2] *Ibid.*, p. 145 f. (English trans., p. 146 f.).

and probably cannot be expressed in words; it is certainly not to be equated with "speech" in the ordinary sense. True communion between persons may take place silently, whereas extreme garrulity may mark the triadic dialectic.[1]

What Marcel calls "judgements in the second person" are not judgements in the usual sense, statements about objects of thought or observation —"information". When I say, "You are good", says Marcel, I express my relation to you, not information about you. (When I tell a woman that her hair looks nice or that she is wearing a pretty dress, she knows I am not simply talking about her hair or her dress, but that I am addressing myself to her.) Personal judgements do not have to do with matters of fact, but with the "global" wholeness of the person. They do not deal with such definite and answerable questions as what the capital of Ghana is, or whether I like pizza, or the colour of someone's skin and hair. Questions about a whole person and his quality, his "virtue" in the traditional sense, transcend the whole realm of question-and-answer thought. Objective, analytical, categorical judgement bears only on *it*, on the unresponsive object of thought which is not really "present" and hence, says Marcel, lacks ontological value. Second-person judgements are a matter of faith and love, of what Marcel calls "credit". The *thou* is present only to one who gives himself, who "gives credit" and believes unconditionally. "Being is truly immanent only for loving thought",[2] where the other is a partner and not an object. Again, *thou*-judgements are

[1] See Martin Buber, *Between Man and Man* (London: Kegan, Paul, 1947), pp. 3 f., 19 f.

[2] *Journal métaphysique*, p. 161 (English trans., p. 162).

intended to be heard and responded to by the other: "Every *thou*-judgement expresses a relation of me to the interlocutor, as well as the will that this relation be known to him."[1] It possesses "finality".

Such judgement is actually "invocation", for we are here in the realm of call-and-response, of "encounter", of intimate "presence". This is an ontological relation of being with being, not a dialectical relation of subject to object. Marcel emphasizes that "The *thou* is to invocation what the object is to judgement", and that "*Thou* is . . . essentially that which can be invoked by me".[2] The *thou*-experience is the experience of "presence", of the immediate "withness" of real being.

Let us pause here to note a few points which should not be neglected if we are to understand Marcel's doctrine of the *I–thou* relation. In the first place, the distinction between *thou* and *it* is not the ordinary distinction between "persons" and 'things". It is rather a distinction between the two basic modes of relation to reality, whether that be personal or not. We may adopt the basic *I–thou* stance toward "things", and we may adopt the basic *I–it* stance toward "persons". We can and we do. Marcel is not as clear about this as Buber is in his work *I and Thou*. Buber points out that it is inherent in our condition to alternate between the two stances, both as regards our relations to "persons" and to "things". The restriction of Marcel's examples to human relationships, however, should not mislead us as to his meaning, for his basic thesis concerns the immediate relation between beings, and he is well aware that being includes both

[1] *Journal métaphysique*, p. 155 (English trans., p. 156).
[2] *Ibid.*, pp. 277, 196 (English trans., pp. 286, 200).

the inanimate and the animate as well as the personal. He admits that we can and do think of other persons as *it*, *he*, or *they*; implicitly, he attributes a certain legitimacy to *it*-judgements about human beings, though he does not specify the limits within which such judgements are valid. Marcel's view of the *thou* does not require the physician, lawyer, or other professional practitioners in human affairs to abandon objective analysis and discrimination, even when concerned with relatives and friends, but it insists that to treat them as mere "cases" does not touch their true being.

That we assume both stances toward persons as well as toward things becomes clear in his description of God as the Absolute *Thou* who alone can never become *he* or *it* for us. "When we speak *of* God, know well that it is not of *God* that we speak."[1] God, in contrast to all other beings, can only be addressed as *Thou*, not judged as *It* or *He*. Faith *or* religious belief, then, is a dialogical relation with the Absolute *Thou*, with the absolutely unbounded and uncircumscribed being that is the goal or medium of all finite love. In this mutual, responsive relation the *I* can freely emerge in its wholeness as it becomes *thou* for God. Belief in God is a *thou*-address that is meant to be heard: "A God whom my belief did not interest would not be God, but a simple metaphysical entity."[2] On the one hand, this "finality" has an element of exclusiveness. Three is a crowd here, as in any *I–thou* relation. No third party can stand outside it to judge it or verify it, or to describe either of the partners or their experience of the relation. The Absolute *Thou* cannot be an objective truth for some

[1] *Journal métaphysique*, p. 158 (English trans., p. 159).
[2] *Ibid.*, p. 153 (English trans., p. 154).

uninvolved "*X*" standing outside the *I–Thou* meeting. This "unverifiability" Marcel holds to be an essential characteristic of all ontological participation. (Doubt, denial, or deception is possible only about *he* or *it*—never about *thou*, for being is inseparable from *thou*.)

But while the Absolute *Thou* possesses the exclusiveness common to all *thou*-relations, it also has the unique character of all-inclusiveness. God is not *Thou* for me alone, nor am I alone *thou* for Him. Indeed, He is only *Thou* for me in a community of all other beings, which I "intend" (direct myself, or tend, toward) when I intend Him. I embrace—not forsake—all others. My relation to the Absolute Thou is not an acosmic one in which I hurdle over a world which is as indifferent to me as I am to it (such a skipping-over can only be a preliminary step to the true religious life and communion). Indeed, *I am* only as other beings count for me, and when I enter into a *thou*-relation with God, I will that all other beings shall be *thou* for Him too. "I hope in Thee *for us*", says Marcel in his later work. Given the concept of a creative and redeeming God, it is, indeed, questionable whether for God anything can be merely "it", absolutely unlovable and irredeemable, a mere datum—one of the empirical facts of life.

The inclusion of all beings and not only human persons and God, in the sphere of the *thou*-relation, of course, raises the problem of how the essential mutuality is possible with the animate and inanimate world. We seem to be outside the limits of any genuine "intention" or "address" at these levels of being. Buber suggests in his little book on the *thou*-relation the possibility of "latency" or "verge" and even of the "pre-threshold" of mutuality in the non-human world.[1] Something is really there for us in our relation to the natural world; beings address themselves and reveal themselves to us—in an ontological sense, below the individual, personal level. After all, the *I–thou* relation is essentially ontological, a matter of the intention of being, and may or may not involve consciousness. It is true that Marcel has neglected the realm of our relations with the natural world in order to concentrate on personal relations—of man to man and of man to God. But it is clear that, for him, no being must be excluded from the *thou*-relation and that we always love a being in God, who is the "absolute recourse" and the ultimate locus of love and all thou-relations. (If we love the world toward God, and in God, then does the "current" flow back toward us, and the world love us back—also toward God?)

Prayer is for Marcel the prime example of the relation to the Absolute *Thou*, of invocation and mutuality. Prayer is not a pragmatic technique, a means of securing our finite ends through the absolute recourse. "In this sense, pragmatism is the negation of all religion."[2] Prayer is a matter of being, and of being-with, not of having. "I can pray to be more, not to have more."[3] Prayer can transform my *being*, but it can add nothing to my *having*—to my finite possessions, "inner" or "outer". It transcends that banal distinction, for it is not a matter of mere subjective "states of soul" as against "material things". It is a matter of being and being-with, of a *we*-community, directed toward

---

[1] See the Postscript to the American edition of *I and Thou* (New York: Charles Scribner's Sons, 1958), esp. pp. 124–126.

[2] *Journal métaphysique*, p. 258 (English trans., p. 266).

[3] *Ibid.*, p. 219 (English trans., p. 224).

the absolute being who is always *thou* and never *it* for us. In this view, intercessory prayer is not only possible, it is necessarily implied. But I cannot pray for another person insofar as he is *it* for me, for his use-value ("O God, I pray Thee to make my servant well so I can receive guests this weekend!"). I can only pray for him, as he is *thou* for me, a real being and self, as *we are* in a spiritual community, as we are we. "There is, at the base of prayer, a will to union with my brothers, without which it would be deprived of all religious value."[1]

Prayer, for Marcel, implies something like the traditional omnicompetence of the divine will expressed in the Biblical phrase, "For God all things are possible." It implies that the world is not set up in a permanent order, a course that runs in pre-established grooves, which the ultimate will cannot change. "To pray is to refuse to admit that all is given; it is to invoke reality treated as will."[2] Prayer has to do with the immediate present, the moment, the once-for-all, the unique now and new. Prayer is renewal, the "active negation of experience", the opposite of passive conformity to the customary way of things. The religious soul re-recognizes no precedents, no established, unquestionable, acquired order. It does recognize an absolute will that transcends all establishments and precedents, that can break in and will uniquely and anew. And it avows an utter dependence on this will, the will of the Absolute *Thou* that wills the person who prays in his incomparable uniqueness, and hence that wills all the things and events of the world in their incomparable uniqueness. The utter dependence implied in prayer is not a matter of

[1] *Journal métaphysique*, p. 258 (English trans., p. 265).
[2] *Ibid.*, p. 219 (English trans., p. 224).

surrender to overwhelming external force or a fatalistic acceptance of an inevitable abstract order. It is a free and spontaneous affirmation within a mutual *I–thou* relation—"*Thy* will be done"—not conformity with an impersonal law or order. Above all, it is not a passive surrender to divine "predestination", which in its commonly understood sense is, for Marcel, a contradiction in terms, for nothing can be absolutely pre-established and inevitable for God. "If I abandon myself entirely to God, it is not to Him that I abandon myself."[1] One of Marcel's plays, *Grace*, includes eloquent warnings against the "temptation" of the "abyss" of predestination.[2]

Like any *I–thou* relation, prayer is not verifiable from the outside, by a detached third party. It is also not verifiable as to its "efficacy" by the person who prays. Marcel insists that the divine response cannot be tested by definite criteria or treated as a causal process. Given the assumed relation, no such question can possibly occur. My prayer is always addressed to that infinite being who is the Absolute *Thou* for me, who cannot fail to hear and understand and respond to my prayer. In this sense, no truly addressed prayer can fail to be efficacious, though not always in an obvious way. Once I inquire about God's attitude and response toward my prayer, I step outside of the *I–thou* relation and transform my prayer into an object, into a not-prayer.

This may seem a circular argument, in which the *I-thou* relation, as immediate experience, is its own proof. In a sense, this is true and has to be so. But

[1] *Journal métaphysique*, p. 259.
[2] Père André warns Gérard: "Beware of the abyss that awaits the predestined" (*Le Seuil Invisible*, p. 107).

prayer involves being-with and a transformation of being, according to Marcel. The sense of the presence of the Absolute *Thou* must be there, and so must the genuine "invocation" by the human person, who enters into and opens himself to the relation. Also there must be some sense of transformation, of real change, of an aid that entirely transcends the kind of aid I can get from other human beings. And although he rules out the attainment of finite goods from the scope of prayer, Marcel is clear that we can pray for the sick and the missing, and for miracles, without, however, *testing* the absolute power we pray to by objective observation and checks.

Another significant instance of the ultimate *I–thou* relation is the experience of suffering, evil, frustration, and contradiction. The religious man sees this experience as a "trial" or "test" that is "sent" from a transcendent realm. Such an understanding is possible only within the personal relation to the Absolute *Thou* (as between Job and God). Trial is not a matter of objective causality, with God as an external agent acting on man as his object, understood retrospectively as a past cause producing a present result. "To think religiously is to think the present under the aspect of divine will"[1]—that is, of the Absolute *Thou*, *Thy* will. The attitude of the religious man (of the Psalmist, for instance)—in the present moment, in immediate experience—is that "I [my life and its trials] am willed *by Thee*".

Again, this attitude is not fatalistic, a surrender to the mere determining power of an omnipotent being who is without care or love. For "trial" may be saving as well as overwhelming. It menaces my being, my integral wholeness, and my faith—

[1] *Journal métaphysique*, p. 229 (English trans., p. 235).

defined as the "power of adherence to being". It involves temptation—to succumb to the "menace" of spiritual annihilation and lostness, of meaninglessness and nihilism, in the face of sorrow and disillusion. But it also involves the possibility of the conservation and transformation of the menaced being, through a self-judgement or self-relation which results in a rediscovery and re-unification of the self. "Trial", with its menace and temptation, forces me to measure myself, to find my own height or depth in urgent action. This happy ending is not a guaranteed result, for trial is not a sure thing; it involves a spiritual "wager". It is not mere play-acting, a predetermined charade, but the real thing, where my soul and very being are "at stake".

This peril of the soul or being is characteristic of human existence, of the whole of life, and begins as soon as I come into existence. Life itself is a trial, testing my being and my adherence to being, my self-maintenance and my relation to ultimate, transcendent reality. The world is so constituted that my soul and my being must be constantly subjected to the corrosive dissolvents of experience and criticism. "To be, means to withstand this test, this progressive dissolution. To deny being would be to claim that nothing can withstand the test."[1] This possibility is the basis both of pessimism and nihilism—which Marcel grants are theoretically legitimate—and of religious existence. "There is religious life only for souls which know themselves menaced", and who, in this critical situation, this unique "condition of the heart", pray that the "stake" be saved.[2] Indeed, the soul, ontologically

[1] *Journal métaphysique*, p. 178 (English trans., p. 180).
[2] *Ibid.*, p. 260 (English trans., p. 268).

45

understood, comes really to be "only on condition of having been saved", on the other side of the "dialectic of experience", of "the trial of life". Trial involves "an act that attains being", and the triumphant endurance and emergence of the innermost, vital, dynamic, active core of the self.[1]

Again, Marcel insists that no one outside the *thou*-relation can understand another person's experience as trial. The affirmation that suffering is a trial is not an objectively valid proposition independent of the sayer and the hearer. But neither is it a merely subjective, arbitrary interpretation, without basis in reality. A special situation and intention of the individual being and soul are indispensable to such an understanding of experience. But this special experience and insight can be shared with others insofar as they participate in it and make it their own; as the trial of another person becomes "ours" and not "his" alone, or "theirs". A special discovery in the spiritual order may be universalized "thanks to the power of sympathy which allows me to imagine and live the experience of my neighbour, of my brother, as my own".[2] On the other hand, to reduce trial to a case of biological adaptation, of psychological self-preservation, or "adjustment" is an utterly erroneous kind of universalization, a vain attempt to understand unique spiritual experience in terms of general objective laws. Here, as in all forms of religious experience, any disjunction between objective facts and subjective disposition, between the universal and the private is utterly inappropriate. The implication that only what is objectively validifiable

[1] *Journal métaphysique*, pp. 282, 179 f. (English trans., pp. 291, 181 f.).
[2] *Ibid.*, p. 200 (English trans., p. 204).

by anyone or everyone (by *n'importe qui*) is real, and that everything else is imaginary, is false.

Our common everyday experience gives the lie to this false disjunction. We all know that there are special, directly untransmittable qualities of concrete experience—the special qualities of an intimately known person or place, for instance. Such qualities are inherent in existence; they are not merely predicates of objective substances. Marcel suggests these examples from intimate personal existence: the house I have lived in with those I love, which is permeated with a special and very real quality or tone; and personal charm, "a certain presence of the person around what he says or does", which is revealed to me in immediate experience. Such qualities are matters neither of mere sentiment nor of objective conception—the attribution of a predicate to a subject. They are known through the meeting or communion between actual beings. *Charm* belongs "to what is most metaphysical in the person, to that irreducible and unobjectifiable quality which is undoubtedly only another aspect of what we call existence".[1] Here reality and appearance are one, and charm is indissociable from the act of charming and the person who is charming.

What is significant about this doctrine of religious experience is that it is the construction of a thinker who, at the time he first sketched it, was not an adherent of any historical faith. This is not the apologetic of a church theologian or of a philosopher committed to a particular religion, attempting to reconcile faith and reason. This is the meditation of a secular, uncommitted philosopher attempting to understand a certain realm or level

[1] *Journal métaphysique*, p. 292 (English trans., p. 301).

47

of human experience, without subjecting it to the universal categories of human reason. Marcel admits that the examples in the above paragraph are "very close to concrete experience, very far from 'rational thought' ".[1] He realizes that experience *per se* is not an absolute indication of the structure and meaning of reality, that it must be interpreted, discriminated, and evaluated. But he proceeds on the assumption that experience "intends" reality—a reality that transcends the mind of the experiencer—and that the intention can be revealed by sensitive, participative interpretation. And he attempts a description of the relation, not of the transcendent reality.

[1] *Journal métaphysique*, p. 290 (English trans., p. 299).

IV

Being: Mystery and Exigence

An interval of eight years elapsed between the publication of the *Metaphysical Journal* (1927) and that of Marcel's next philosophical work *Being and Having* (1935). This period was decisive for Marcel's philosophical development. *Being and Having*, which Marcel calls his "hinge-work", introduces us to the unique tone and colour that characterize his later works; in it we first encounter his basic intuitions of human existence and his method of developing and expressing them. Important too is the meditation called "Concrete Approaches to the Ontological Mystery", which first appeared as the epilogue to Marcel's play *The Broken World* in 1933. It presents us with the most concentrated, lucid, and rounded exposition of his later thought; it is in effect a concise summary of and commentary on the themes broached in *Being and Having*. Marcel's later works in the '40's and '50's fill out and enrich these basic themes.

This important and intensely creative period came after a number of years when Marcel did almost no philosophical or dramatic writing (1923–1928)[1]; these years were marked, however, by prolific critical activity which produced an extraordinary number of pieces on drama, literature, and music. The vigorous exercise of Marcel's

---

[1] The last entries in the *Metaphysical Journal* were made in 1923. To it was appended one of the rare philosophical essays of the fallow period, "Existence and Objectivity" (1925).

aesthetic sensibility and interpretative powers in
practical criticism in these fallow years may have
contributed to the richness and deftness of interpretation in his later philosophical works.

A decisive event marked Marcel's resump-
tion of philosophical work: his conversion to the
Catholic faith in his fortieth year. This event
was the culmination of a long, circuitous journey,
starting from a non-religious family background
and a secular philosophical training, proceeding
through the intense and patient inquiries recorded
in the metaphysical journals, and ending in com-
plete acceptance of traditional Christian faith.
The entries in the *Metaphysical Journal* reveal some
of the steps on the way: the search for the mode in
which the mind may grasp immediate existence and
the concrete faith relation—a purely philosophical
search without personal commitment to any particular faith; the salient meditations on the *I–thou*
relation, especially the relation to the Absolute
Thou; and the various inquiries into concrete religious experience.

Marcel came to realize that it was specifically
Christian faith that his inquiries were concerned
with. At first he was more attracted to Protes-
tantism than to Catholicism, impelled by his nonconformist attitude, his need for intellectual
freedom, and his close ties by marriage to a good
Protestant family. A seemingly slight incident
revealed to him his unconscious intention, the
inner requirement (or "exigence"), that he "had
to choose" Catholicism: Marcel's review of a work
by the Catholic writer François Mauriac (*Dieu et
mammon*) elicited a friendly letter from Mauriac,
ending with the query: "But, then, why aren't you
one of us?" These words set going a spiritual ex-

perience which is recorded in the most touching passages in Marcel's journals. They tell of his happiness and peace at the moment of decision, the sense of new birth, of a whole new world opening up before him; then of the days of darkness and doubt as he balks at accepting the catechetical statements, followed by his decision to accept them unreservedly for Christ's sake; and finally of the act and state of baptism, on March 23, 1929. The entry for that day notes: "No exaltation, but a feeling of peace, of balance, of hope, of faith." Of this event Roger Troisfontaines says that Marcel had "encountered God in the Catholic Church" and "engaged himself irrevocably".[1]

The result of this "turning" for Marcel's philosophical thought was not a descent to a sentimental bathos of sweetness and light, nor an optimistic complacency about the human situation. On the contrary, it is in his writings after the conversion event that we get the most cogent expression of his preoccupation with anxiety, despair, betrayal, and suicide—those terrible possibilities and temptations which the new Christian recognizes to be inherent in the very structure of our world. He had already vividly expressed this "realistic" vision of human existence in his plays, especially in those published in *The Invisible Threshold*, *Trois Pièces*, *The Heart of Others*, and *The Iconoclast*. The negative aspects of human experience already voiced there had now to be taken into account in Marcel's philosophical description and interpretation of human existence, of man's being in the world—but they were to

[1] See journal entries in *Être et avoir*, pp. 17, 29 f. (English trans., pp. 15, 23 f.); and Roger Troisfontaines: *De l'existence à l'être: la philosophie de Gabriel Marcel*. Louvain: Nauwelaerts, 1953, and Paris: Vrin, 1953, Vol. I, p. 23 f.

sound different. Some of the most poignant expressions of emptiness and despair in Marcel's journals were written after his conversion—but the tone is no longer stark and unrelieved. Everything is said now within the fundamental context of hope. This theological virtue becomes a dominant theme of Marcel's thought. Hope and faith—in the concrete situation of everyday existence—become the major subjects of his phenomenological interpretations.

Marcel might also be called a "realist" in another sense. His main concern now is with man's relation to "the real", to being, rather than with the modes by which the mind may grasp certain levels of experience. His interest has become ontological rather than epistemological, and he has finally emerged from his idealist beginnings. Marcel's approach to being, however, is not the traditional one, which directs the mind to the highest level of abstraction. He deals rather with particular, concrete elements and situations in human existence, instead of with Being with a capital "B". Marcel acknowledges the bewilderment that the odd phrase "concrete approaches to the ontological mystery" must arouse among professional philosophers. Thinkers interested in "concrete approaches" often regard being as a meaningless term, while those who take being seriously do not usually care for "concrete approaches". Furthermore, being is not a "mystery" to conventional ontological thinkers, but something which can be grasped by the human mind; whereas "mystery" for them connotes the Holy, the supernatural realm.

However, in *Being and Having* Marcel begins his discussion of the relation between thought and being, and of the relation of particular existence to being, in accord with traditional realism: Thought bears on being, on something beyond the mind and its ideas; it is not self-relation but self-transcendence. Thought, says Marcel, is "turned toward the Other". Thought intends and "requires" being, which is the "magnet" that draws it out. But, granted that when we think, we intend something beyond our thought, why speak of "being" in the singular, and even with a capital letter? Why not say "beings", referring to the particular things or existences that our thought bears on in our common experience? Marcel agrees that thought bears on concrete, particular existence, but he insists that finite, contingent existence—what "exists", what stands forth—points to or intends ultimate, infinite being.

Many themes are pursued in Marcel's speculations on this subject.[1] He considers a contemporary Thomistic argument that the principle of identity or self-contradiction demonstrates that there is such a thing as "being in itself" or "being in general". In this view, it is a consequence of the structure of reality, not merely of the rules of the game of thought, that something cannot both be and not be at the same time, cannot both be what it is and not be what it is. If we deny the principle of identity, Marcel speculates, then we must have recourse to some form of relativism which asserts that particular beings exist, but not being in general, or to a pure nominalism which denies that the term "being" has any meaning, or to an idealism which separates thought from its objective referent. We would end up, then, with a basically meaningless

[1] See especially the journal entries in *Être et avoir* from June 12 to August 9, 1929.

and incoherent world or with a thought that has been reduced to a kind of dream.

Marcel is not happy, however, about the term "being in general". He is quick to point out that the absolute being which is indicated by the principle of identity cannot be pure indeterminacy, an absolute void without individual characteristics. If it were, how could we establish any connection between our thoughts about finite, conditional beings and being itself? Marcel suggests that we consider the infinite, ultimate reality as an *ens realissimus*, a perfectly real and fully determinate being, "an absolute structure which would be at the same time an absolute life"; that is, a "positive infinite", a completely full reality, in which every finite being, with all its distinctive characteristics, participates.

Interspersed with these abstract and abstruse speculations, which follow clues provided by traditional thought, are meditations which prepare the way for Marcel's "concrete approaches" to the mystery of being. For example, in discussing the relation between thought and existence, he asserts that thought cannot be separated from existence and put on some higher "essential" plane, for thought is itself on the existential plane, is "inside existence". The thought we always have to do with is the thought of an existing thinker, which may be abstracted from existence for a specific purpose, but cannot be reduced to "pure thought" save at the price of a crippling "lie" or "blindness". And a mind thus maimed and darkened cannot deal with actual existence.

Marcel also introduces a significant distinction between the thought that binds beings together or beings to being, and the thought that recognizes or

constructs essences, structures, and ideas. The first
type of thought, which he calls "thinking *of*" (on
the analogy of the German terms *andenken*, for
"remember", and *Andacht*, for "devotion"), bears
on real beings and events, depends on a particular
context, and establishes a community or "withness"
of beings. The second type of thought, which he
calls simply "thinking", bears on structures and
essences; it is impersonal and independent of a
particular community.[1] Marcel stresses the decisive importance of the first type, "thinking of",
particularly in the realm between persons or subjects, or more exactly between *I* and *thou*. In treat-
ing the other as *thou*, he says, "I penetrate more
deeply into him, and apprehend his being or his
essence more directly" than when I treat him as *he*.
Marcel gives a new turn to the meaning of "essence" in the case of human beings: my essence is
not only my "nature", permanent and unalterable,
but also *my freedom not to be what I am*, "quite simply
to be able to betray myself", to negate myself.[2]

It is this essence as freedom that I encounter
when I treat the other person as *thou*; indeed, by so
doing I help him to become free, to become his
essence as freedom—this is what happens in love.
Moreover, it is only when he is free that he is really
"other"; as nature, he is the same as I.

> The other *qua* other exists for me only insofar as
> I am open to him (as he is a *thou*), but I am open
> to him only insofar as I cease to form a closed
> circle with myself, inside which I somehow put
> the other, or rather the idea of him; for in rela-
> tion to this circle the other becomes merely my

[1] *Être et avoir*, pp. 40–43 (English trans., p. 31 f.).
[2] *Ibid.*, pp. 153 f. (English trans., p. 106).

idea of the other—and the idea of the other is no longer the other *qua* other, it is the other insofar as related to me, displaced and disintegrated . . .[1]

This "thinking of" the other person as *thou*, this loving knowledge of our fellows, is familiar to us in our everyday experience, but how are we to think *of* infinite being? How can we know anything about the ultimate reality beyond conceptual thought and existential experience? Marcel answers that such knowledge is a matter of being-with, of ontological participation, and that it follows from our situation of being in the world. Our original and basic situation is that *we are engaged in being*, that *we are*. Our spiritual task is to affirm our being and the "plenary reality" in which we participate. The problem of being is a very peculiar one, for *we are what we are inquiring about*, we are what we affirm. Indeed, precisely speaking, being is not a "problem", to be analysed and solved, but a "mystery" to be recognized and realized. It belongs, says Marcel, to the realm of the "meta-problematic".

> A problem is something which is encountered, which bars the way. It lies entirely before me. Mystery, on the contrary, is something in which I find myself engaged, whose essence it is, consequently, not to be entirely before me. It is as if in this zone the distinction of "in me" and "before me" loses its meaning.[2]

The recognition of ontological mystery is bound up with personal involvement in being, with the

[1] *Être et avoir*, p. 155 (English trans., p. 107).

[2] *Ibid.*, p. 145 (English trans., p. 100). See also the etymology of the term "problem".

"ontological status" of the self that has itself raised the question of being.

> I who inquire about being do not know firstly whether I am, nor *a fortiori what* I am—nor even quite clearly what this question 'What am I?' means, though it still obsesses me. *Thus we see the problem of being encroaching on its own data; it is pursued inside the subject who propounds it.* It is therewith denied (or transcended) as problem and transformed into mystery.[1]

"I" and "am" are inseparable, and the affirmation of my wholeness, of my full reality, involves the affirmation of the wholeness of being. I affirm being as a participant therein—I do not pronounce on it from the outside—in an "affirmation *which I am rather than pronounce . . . and of which I am rather the seat than the subject*".[2] Thus the dualism between the self which affirms being, and the being which is affirmed by it, is transcended, and knowledge, as participation in being, becomes itself a metaproblematic mystery. In this view, if we may use a clumsy coinage, being is "*is*-ed" rather than said.

Marcel opposes the mystery of being to the merely and purely natural, the *tout naturel*. He suggests that our very condition requires us to shut off the mystery in and around us and live in the objective, natural world—that it may be the essence of objects, of mere things, to shut off the mystery. Hence, in order to attain being we must break through the shell we have secreted around ourselves and transcend our condition. "Ontological exigence" is the quest for participation in

---

[1] *Être et avoir*, p. 169 (English trans., p. 117).
[2] *Mystère ontologique*, p. 56 (English trans., p. 8).

57

the transcendent ground of our personal reality. It is an absolute human requirement, a need, a thirst, a hunger. "I *avidly aspire* to participate in this being, in this reality",[1] in this plenary presence, says Marcel.

But we are not in being as beans in a bowl—supinely, automatically, passively. We must affirm —or deny—our being in being. This affirmation or recognition comes through re-collection, the "ontological index" par excellence. In this act I withdraw from ordinary experience to re-collect myself, to regain my personal unity. There is something in me which is not identical with my life, something which I grasp or open myself to at the moment of recollection, but it is not to myself, in the limited sense, that I withdraw in recollection, but to my being with being. It is very hard to describe this act in traditional philosophical language. Marcel has recourse to a dramatic description of what he considers the most dramatic moment in the rhythm of consciousness. He seizes on the disjuncture between "my being" and "my life" that is implied in the very act of recollection, and points to my capacity to stand over against my own life, to confront it and to judge it, and hence to affirm or destroy it.

The possibility of suicide, despair, and betrayal is involved in the very structure of our universe, of which dissolution and death are constituent elements. These negative aspects, however, can be transcended through fidelity, hope, and love. It is in the elucidation of these spiritual data that we must seek the "concrete approaches to the ontological mystery". Says Marcel, . . .

[1] *Mystère ontologique*, p. 51 (English trans., p. 5)—my italics.

the ontological order can be recognized personally only by the whole of a being engaged in a drama which is his own, while yet surpassing him infinitely in every sense; a being to whom has been imparted the singular power of affirming or denying himself, inasmuch as he affirms being and opens himself to it—or as he denies it and thereby closes himself: for it is in this dilemma that there lies the very essence of freedom.[1]

Thus the possibility of negation and the possibility of affirmation are mutually implied in the structure of our world; ontological exigence and ontological experience arise out of this basic situation. The true philosopher, the real metaphysician, will take his stand here, in this basic human drama, amid "these tragic data of human life". We may temporarily seek refuge from these primal confrontations in ideal, impersonal truths or in the world of problems and techniques, where there is no place for mystery or presence (no being over against us), but in the end it is precisely such solutions which lead to emptiness, despair, and meaninglessness.

These reflections and insights link up with those of the *Metaphysical Journal* on the "risk" or "stake" of human existence, on the possibility of "perdition" and hence of salvation. The "menace" of non-being, involved in man's situation, arouses in him the ontological exigence. In a time like our own, when that situation and its attendant danger are starkly revealed, this need or hunger for being becomes acute. It is the integral wholeness of the person, it is the soul that can be lost, that is menaced. It is of the essence of the human soul that it

[1] *Être et avoir*, p. 175 (English trans., p. 120 f.).

can be saved or lost, and this is a matter of being. That my life can appear meaningless is an integral part of its structure, and is bound up with its meaningfulness. But the losing or saving of being is not just a passive happening; it involves will—the will to be saved or destroyed—for there is a will to destruction, of self or others, and our world is so made that we may desert it by "getting rid of" ourselves. But this is *not* an "absolute desertion" of being unless my being and my life are the same, both coming to an end in death, and this Marcel trenchantly denies.

The "broken world" passage in the play to which Marcel appended his meditation on the ontological mystery conveys to us vividly the sense of a world where human existence has lost its "ontological weight", of a meaningless life and an empty world. The play centres around a charming woman who leads an aimless life, with despairing insight into its emptiness, and her desperate attempts to build some solid relations. She lives in a world of fake art and fake love, of false relations, where anything goes and nothing satisfies. She says to a friend:

Don't you sometimes have the impression that we are living . . . if that can be called living . . . in a broken world? Yes, broken as a broken watch. The spring does not work any more. In appearance nothing has changed. Everything is in its proper place. But if one puts the watch to one's ear . . . one no longer hears anything. You understand, the world, what we call the world, the world of men . . . formerly it must have had a heart. But it's as if the heart has ceased to beat.[1]

[1] *Le Monde cassé*, p. 44.

The "broken world" is a world without unity or community: everyone goes on about his own affairs, without real communication, without real meeting. There are merely chance collisions. "There is no longer a centre, no longer a life, anywhere," says the despairing lady. But she keeps listening, listening "into the void". The possibility of salvation, of attaining the fullness of reality, comes to her through a message of communion and sustaining presence from a beloved friend who has died, from one *beyond* life, and as the play ends she seeks to bring the light of this encounter into the common, daily life of herself and her husband.

V

Being and Having

As in his early meditations on ontological participation Marcel distinguished between existence and objectivity, so in his middle period he contrasts being and having. In the *Metaphysical Journal* this distinction was made in terms of feeling: the difference between the finite, transmittable feelings which I *have*, and the "global" reality of the feeling that I *am*. The contrast now is stated in terms of man's situation in the world and of his ontological exigence, and its fulfillment or frustration. The emphasis on the body in the early journal is reiterated and related to the unity (but not identity) of self and body, the "global" wholeness of my being and my life, and to the basic question, "What am I?" "My body", earlier seen as the typical form of existence, is now seen as the typical form of having. It is the "absolute having", the basis of all having, which cannot itself be had, annexed, or disposed of, because it "encroaches" on me, on my being. This "encroachment" is basic to my human and creaturely situation. My being is hidden, shut off from consciousness by my life and my body, by my incarnate existence, which cannot be a datum or object for me—I cannot stand outside it, I am involved in it, I am it. More exactly, corporality is on the frontier between being and having; "my body" does and does not belong to me; I can and cannot dispose of it, for I can dispose of it absolutely only by making it absolutely "indisposable" (unavailable)—by committing suicide.

Hence Marcel is not inclined to see the distinction between being and having as that between the spiritual and the physical—to accept the easy solution that I "am" myself, but that I "have" a body. My body is essential to my having, to my possession of what is outside me—it is through my body that I have; but having implies being, as possession implies a possessor, and contents a container. Thus having and being are interdependent but distinct. They are mutually illuminating, and we may come to an understanding of being through an understanding of having. "It might be," suggests Marcel, "that a phenomenological analysis of having would constitute a useful introduction to a renewed analysis of being. By phenomenological analysis I mean the analysis of an implicit content of thought, in opposition to a psychological analysis bearing on *states*."[1] This is the analysis that Marcel attempts in the "Sketch of a Phenomenology of Having", which is included in *Being and Having*. In it, he reveals the peculiar tension, insecurity, and obsession that is involved in having and how it may be counteracted by the creative spirit.

Having, he says in this piece, is always obsessed with the other as *it*, not as *thou*. The basic intention of having is to take in what is other, to hold on to it, to keep accumulating, and never to let go. Hence the basic tension in having between possessor and possessions, the fear of loss, the sense of menace by the ocean of otherness, and the vain attempt to incorporate possessions into the self. What can be kept in can also be taken away; hence the pain of

[1] *Être et avoir*, p. 219 (English trans., p. 151).

63

possible loss of what one has and the pain of covetousness for what does not have. "To desire is in some way to have without having,"[1] says Marcel. A vicious dialectic ensues whereby the possessor becomes the possessed: my "attachment" of things to myself also attaches me to them and gives them the power to absorb and annihilate me—my having devours my being. But a counter-dialectic is possible that may transform having into being through creative activity and love; the tense duality of possessor and possessed may be transformed into the being-with of *I* and *thou*.

What is had (unlike what is) can be characterized: it is *cernible* and *discernible*—it can be encompassed and distinguished. But any characterization involves falsification, for others *are* too, are beings, not mere items for my thought: "Characterization is a certain mode of possessing, or claiming to possess, the unpossessable."[2] Indeed, a double falsification takes place, involving both the characterizer and the characterized. For other reality can be characterized only "insofar as we cut ourselves off from it, and hence desert ourselves". This double falsification requires a double transformation to restore the other reality (that we have reduced to a mere reference point) and thus to restore us to ourselves. In bearing on the reality or being of others we attain our own.

It goes without saying that having is not merely a matter of material possessions. The whole realm of academic scholarship, the various mental disciplines and techniques (theoretical and practical), the "communications" industry, all our political and economic apparatus and knowledge—all these

[1] *Être et avoir*, p. 236 (English trans., p. 162).
[2] *Ibid.*, p. 246 f. (English trans., p. 169).

64

belong to the realm of having. These activities are marked by abstraction, specialization (alienation), and autonomy;[1] and their products may be even more possessive of their possessors than material gains. As a counter-balance to these autonomous precise disciplines of what can be managed and had, Marcel points to those non-autonomous activities centred on being: religion, art, and metaphysics. These are "the central activities by which man is recalled to the presence of the mystery which is his foundation and apart from which he is only nothingness".[2]

Marcel proceeds to an interpretation of the basic situations of human existence in terms of the rhythm of being and having. He picks out two moments in the self's participation in being: "disposability" and "engagement". Disposability (or availability) is the capacity to be present or open to being or to other beings. Its opposite, "indisposability" (or unavailability), is characterized by a holding-back, self-adherence, closed-in-ness (something like Kierkegaard's *Indesluttedhed*, or "shut-in-ness"). Whereas the disposable person opens freely and gives himself unreservedly to a "withness" of being and a mutuality of presence, the indisposable person is self-preoccupied, self-

[1] For Marcel, "autonomy", the self-determination of the will, is not the shibboleth of freedom, as in the Kantian ethics, but marks instead the sphere of techniques, abstractions, and specialization, in which man may become enslaved to the part of the self which has become mortified and alienated through these processes. Autonomous activities involve only a part of the self and operate in a limited and controllable area; non-autonomous activities enlist the whole of the self and are rooted in being itself, in the open and unlimited. This involvement in being transcends the destructive tension between the self and the other and bestows true freedom.

[2] *Ibid.*, p. 255 (English trans., p. 175).

encumbered, self-enclosed, incapable of giving himself, of opening up, of giving out. If he listens to me, he gives me only his ear, the outward attitude, but he refuses me himself, for he cannot "make room" for anyone else in himself.

Marcel sketches an "egocentric topography" of the heart, which he sees as prudently divided into zones of decreasing interest and adherence, with oneself at the centre, safe and secure, and an interest in others only as they are close to No. 1 and his interests. (Fielding's Tom Jones and young Blifil are good examples of disposability and indisposability, respectively.) This parochialism of the soul prevents us from really believing and accepting the reality of other beings. But these hedgehog defences may be pierced by a sudden encounter with a stranger that moves us so deeply that it becomes an "appeal" to which we must respond. In such an encounter the other who has been far away becomes close to us, the self is no longer the centre of our universe, and we realize that "we are not our own".

Indisposability is marked by having, the tendency to identify oneself with what one has, to be possessed by one's possessions. This is not so much a material having as a preoccupation with one's own life, talents, qualities, and status—it is one's self that is had and cannot be given up. Indisposability means "self-preoccupation", which is occupation *in a certain way*, not with a certain object.

Laurent Chesnay in *The Broken World* is a man self-encumbered, beset with *amour-prôpre*, unable to get in touch with others; and Antonov in the same play, who throws himself at others, encumbers others with himself, is in no better state. Neither of these self-imprisoned souls intends the other as other. In the Marcellian psychoanalysis, such a person feels compressed to the point of explosion, like a vast volume of gas forced into a small space. There is a paradoxical conjuncture of constriction and agitation, a boundless disquietude at the core of a rigid fixation. As the personal being is stifled through "closed-in-ness" and self-encumbrance, a boundless anxiety ensues that is not evoked by any particular object. This disquietude is for Marcel the anxiety of temporality, of being a prey to time, of being consumed and macerated by existence. It calls forth "un-hope" (after Thomas Hardy), which becomes despair when it is related to a determinate object.

Two vivid passages from the journal entries in *Being and Having* give us a concrete sense of what Marcel means by this boundless anxiety. In one place he writes:

> What I have called anxiety as a fundamental human deformity, as a . . . universal datum. . . . The most vivid image of it I can think of is the horrible feeling I have sometimes had in the dark of being delivered up to darkness, with nothing to hold on to.[1]

And in a passage written on a gloomy Sunday he notes:

> Time as opening out on death—upon my death —upon my *loss*. The time-abyss; dizziness in the presence of this time at the bottom of which is my death and which sucks me in.[2]

Thus indisposability ends in utter hopelessness and dread. But out of this despair, or the situation

[1] *Ibid.*, p. 107 (English trans., p. 74).
[2] *Ibid.*, p. 117 (English trans., p. 117).

that calls forth despair, may come hope; out of in-disposability may come disposability. Hope starts from a situation which invites us to despair and to give way to a pessimistic fatalism, a *mistrust*, which sees reality as uninterested or impotent in effecting our good or any absolute good, as something in which we put no *credit*. Hope puts trust in reality, in the totality of being, trust that it will ultimately overcome the danger and the imminent loss, trust that there is something in it which wills what I will when I will the good with all my being. "It [hope] is always directed toward the restoration of a cer-tain living order in its integrity. But on the other hand, it includes the affirmation of eternity, of eternal goods . . . all hope is hope of salvation"[1] (In a later piece Marcel says: "All hope is hope of resurrection."[2])

This implies a world of real "lesions", where the living order has been morbidly damaged, and also a world where "miracles" are possible. It also im-plies a world with an invisible realm, where hope is fulfilled and "integrity" restored, like that realm of the "unverifiable" of previous meditations, where man's prayers bear fruit. This is a realm beyond our control, beyond all technique, calculation, and doing. Hope is an act of *non-doing*, with its "springs" in the invisible world. It involves the "radical re-fusal to calculate possibilities", as if it were in touch with a principle at the heart of things and events which make all such calculations ridiculous. It is an appeal to that ally who is Love. But it is also *will*, in the sense of prophetic affirma-tion or vision ("This will be, it shall come to

[1] *Être et avoir*, p. 108f. (English trans. p. 75).
[2] "Structure de l'espérance," *Dieu Vivant*, No. 19 (1951), p. 78.

68

pass"), a will whose point of application is infinity, eternity.

> Metaphysically speaking, *the sole authentic hope is that which rests on what does not depend on us.* . . .
> Hope seems to me like the prolongation into the unknown of a central activity, that is, one rooted in being. Hence, its affinities, not indeed with desire, but with will. The will, too, in fact, involves a refusal to calculate possibilities, or at least a halt in such calculation. Thus, could not hope be defined as a will bearing on what does not depend on it?[1]

On this basis, we must distinguish between the selfish "claim" in the realm of having and the authentic hope that waits on the grace of a beneficent power beyond us; we must differentiate between self-centred desire and an openness to being. "Hope is to desire what patience is to passivity."[2]

Hope and life go together (if life is understood in the ontological sense), and the soul stands between them. It is the soul, we recall, that is at stake, that can be lost or saved; and life always has an "animic index", or mark of the soul, when it is the life of a *thou*. Hope, then, is the breath of the soul, and we are stifled without it. But we can choose to be asphyxiated, we can exist in a state of self-contradiction; for although "living, for man, is to accept life, to say yes to life", we can say "no" to it, we can deny our being. We can, as Ivan Karamazov says, "turn in our ticket". Thus, despair is possible, and that man may embrace his own death, his own destruction, his own nullification, is for

[1] *Mystère ontologique*, pp. 73, 75 (English trans., pp. 19, 20).
[2] *Être et avoir*, p. 131, n. 1, and p. 135 (English trans., p. 91, n. 1, and p. 93).

Marcel a "central datum for metaphysics", which must take its stand in the face of human despair and fulfil the "necessity to restore to human experience its ontological weight".

Ontological communion, the self's participation in being, or being-with, comprises two moments: opening-up and entering-in, or, in Marcel's lexicon, "disposability" and "engagement". The latter term connotes both involvement (being taken into) and commitment (giving oneself up to). In *Being and Having*, "engagement" becomes practically a synonym, deeply enriched in meaning, for the "participation" of the *Metaphysical Journal*. Ontological communion is now seen in the light of the basic dispositions and actions of "fidelity", "promise", and "witness".

Marcel's phenomenological analysis discerns two basic marks of engagement: that it is absolutely unconditional and that it intends other reality. Engagement does not depend on my momentary mental states, feelings, or disposition. When I engage myself, I engage myself once for all, come what come may. My engagement transcends all variations of mood and circumstance (leaving aside purely external physical hindrances). When I commit myself, I commit my future (which, of course, I cannot know beforehand), I assert the continuity of my will and intention, and I maintain the unity and identity of my present and future self. But such an affirmation discloses a turning toward other beings or being; commitment is not self-centred or self-regarding. I commit myself to another being—not to myself, or my word, or my honour, and certainly not to an abstract principle or an impersonal ideal, but always to a being who is *thou* for me, who is really *other* for me. Engagement is not "gratuitous", a matter of my arbitrary whim or say-so, but is always the response to another and refers to the "hold" of other reality over me. Engagement—in the absolutely unconditional sense—is contracted by my whole self and addressed to the whole of being and is made in its presence. All fidelity to a being is ultimately grounded in being itself, or, in religious terms, in the commitment to God and the "hold" of God over me. All engagement is "before God".

Marcel's favourite example of the absolute unconditionality of engagement is the promise a man makes to a mortally sick friend to visit him again. When he makes the promise he is moved by pity and good intentions, but when the time for the promised visit approaches he does not feel the same; he is even annoyed that he made the promise at all. Perhaps he does not feel sympathetic and outgoing at the moment, and he would rather stay home or find some cheerful amusement. But he did promise, he did commit himself—not to feel the same, but to make the visit, to be with his friend. A promise involves a decision not to be influenced by changes in mood and situation; it has the power to abstract from all such changes. When I promise, I bind myself absolutely; I decree that my promise be absolutely unconditional—"come what come may" —and I will have no qualms about a specious "sincerity" or a false fidelity to my state of mind at some future moment, when the promised act is to be performed. When I promise, I give myself absolutely; my word is my bond, my *religio*. There is a supra-temporal identity of the self which transcends all temporary states, a being which must be maintained against the flux of becoming.[1]

[1] *Être et avoir*, pp. 56–80 (English trans., pp. 41–56). This is one of the richest passages in the *Journals*.

As disposability is expressed in hope, so engagement is expressed in fidelity. These are the ontological acts *par excellence*. Being is "the place of fidelity". Fidelity is a creative attestation of being, the "perpetuation of witness". As Nietzsche said that man was the animal who can promise, Marcel says that man is essentially "a being who can bear witness". Witness bears on being itself, is justifiable only as it refers to permanent being, and would be impossible in a world of discrete moments of experience. It involves memory, "the ontological sign"—when I bear false witness I betray being. Witness is a creative act of participation and self-giving, an active response which we may make or refuse to make, even though such refusal means our self-negation. For fidelity is creative action, not supine obedience, inert routine, or habitual "observance". It is the active affirmation or recognition of ontological permanence, the "perpetuation of presence" (of a being as present to me—I constantly maintain the sick friend's presence, which does not depend on sight and sound); fidelity requires that I keep myself open to other reality.[1]

All of the above description of ontological experience, of the self's disposability to and engagement in being, bears on religious faith. Indeed, for Marcel, absolute engagement is faith, and faith is "perpetual witness" to transcendent reality, that is, absolute fidelity. The "martyrs" of faith are the paradigmatic witnesses. As thought intends being, so faith bears on reality—it is not an expression of private sentiment. Worship is an act of disposa-

---

[1] *Être et avoir*, pp. 55, 137–144, 314–316 (English trans., pp. 41, 95–100, 214 f.); *Mystère ontologique*, pp. 76–82 (English trans., pp. 21–25); "Testimony and Existentialism", in *The Philosophy of Existence*, pp. 67–76.

bility to and engagement in other reality. The self is opened and offered to a transcendent reality which cannot be grasped—as symbolized in the joined hands of prayer, which indicate that the person forswears all handling or grasping for the act of dedication and devotion. Marcel sees the decay of religious faith in the modern world as connected with the rationalist and idealist weakening of the ontological sense, and the resultant loss of being, and hence of humanity, in modern man. He looks to the restoration of the primordial natural trust in being, of the ancient bond between man and the universe, natural piety, to repair the damage to man's integrity and sense of reality. He calls for an "immense work of critical reconstruction" that will reveal the underlying assumptions of "a thought which, after having despoiled the mind of its attributes and of its ontological capacity, nevertheless confers upon the mind some of the most dreadful prerogatives of That One whom it imagines it has dethroned".[1]

[1] *Être et avoir*, p. 357 (English trans., p. 240).

VI

Existence: Person and Community

Marcel's interpretation of human existence rests
on his analysis of man's participation in being.
Human existence is understood in terms of ontological exigence, disposability, and engagement—as
the fulfilment or frustration of participation in
being. Conversely, man's participation in being
and his relation to God is understood through a
discernment of the intention of the basic acts of
human existence. Indeed, Marcel insists that any
philosophical knowledge of reality must begin with
an immersion in the basic "trials" and "situations"
of human existence.

Start from the concrete human condition, he
advises, that is, from your own finite existential
situation, from your partial perspective of the
world, and deepen your sense of that condition.
Do not try to take refuge in some thought-in-
general (in *Denken überhaupt*), or to place yourself at
the imaginary standpoint of an impersonal Absolute, or to sacrifice concrete life and reality to the
idol of objective validity and verifiability. Such
depersonalized thought grasps neither existence nor
transcendence and is irrelevant to the eternal
questions of man's condition and destiny.

Religious experience—man's relation to ultimate
reality—can be understood through a sensitive
interpretation of the basic conditions and situations
of human existence. And to know what man is we
must first understand those basic experiences which

are essentially religious, such as trust, loyalty, sacrifice, promise, and witness. A basic community of human experience underlies religious insight and experience: the universal human consciousness of participating in a common adventure and destiny, of sharing in a common experience of suffering, love, and the stages on life's way. This "incarnate community" of basic experiences—before religion and apart from religion—provides the "concrete foundations" of the religious consciousness. It is the zone of human nature where authentic religious life may emerge, the zone of "creative attestation", where the human person bears witness to the presence of being.

Marcel's interpretation of human existence was set forth in the cataclysmic period which saw the rise of Hitler and the Nazi subjugation of France and Europe. The "Introduction" to *From Refusal to Invocation* (1940) speaks "from the threshold of the catacombs" and envisages an imminent struggle against "the denial of man by man, or, more profoundly, of the more-than-human by the less-than-human".[1] The pieces in *Homo Viator* (1944), which sound the themes of exile, captivity, alienation, separation, hope, and fidelity were addressed, often by word of mouth, to an audience that was undergoing the German occupation and the Vichy régime. The state of the world gave a dramatic urgency to these pieces written between 1935 and 1944 and provided a concrete, historical community of experience as the basis for understanding insights that Marcel had explored in his earlier meditations.

A careful reading of Marcel's early works demonstrates that these later pieces were no mere oppor-

[1] *Du Refus à l'invocation*, p. 16 f.

75

tunistic pamphleteering, in step with the times, and that his emphasis on personal existence was not a mimicking of an ephemeral intellectual fashion. His quest for participation in being, recorded in the *Metaphysical Journal*, dates back to the 'teens of this century, and his early paper on *Existence and Objectivity* (1925) long antedates the rise of "existentialism" in France. Marcel's existential thought differs from that of his younger contemporaries, who had a sensational éclat in the '40's and '50's, by its hopeful, theocentric character. Robert Campbell once noted, perhaps with some exaggeration, that this "oldest of the French existentialist thinkers" was the only one who was not an atheist. Despite his continual emphasis on the negativities of human existence, Marcel opposes the view that man is alien and alone in the world, "condemned to be free", or has been "thrown" into existence. Furthermore, Marcel's thought is an expression of his existential experience rather than an attempt to make an objective system of existence. Following Berdyaev's distinction, Marcel is an "existential philosopher" rather than a "philosopher of existence"—he belongs with Kierkegaard rather than with Heidegger.

We may, however, discern these main themes in Marcel's interpretation of human existence:

(*a*) The basic condition of human existence is that it is *incarnate*. I exist as "my body". I am present to and participate in the world through my body and my feeling, and it is only in this way that the world is present to me, that it exists for me. This is the fundamental, irreducible condition which is the ground of all fact for us. "My body" is the centre of the existential orbit and the central datum or "marker" for metaphysics. Everything basically human is bound up with this situation, and existentially I cannot get out of it, cannot transcend it, although I may refuse to recognize it and may abstract myself away from it in thought. That I am here as this particular body is basic to my existence, not a mere contingency. I and my body are at one. I cannot have existed as some other body.

(b) It is also a basic condition of human existence that it resides in a *particular situation.* "The essence of man is to be in a situation,"[1] says Marcel. This is not merely a matter of physical and temporal location. To be "in a situation" means to be placed in a specific and concretely qualified mode, in an internally qualified and dynamic life-connection that cannot be reduced to abstract terms. "Situation" is not a matter of simple location, but connotes value, involvement, and vulnerability. For instance, we talk of a place being "badly" situated or of men being situated "between" places, forces, or realms; and our common speech is full of metaphors—"at the end (or edge) of", "above" or "beyond", "beneath" and "besides"—that denote qualified situations, not spatial determinations. We are not merely there-at, but also there-between and there-with.

Being in a situation involves being vulnerable to all that which surrounds us—vulnerable and fulfillable. In our individual existence we are incomplete, inchoate, and inconsistent, and we need to be completed through the inflowing ambiance or "in-fluence" of the world. Such completion requires an active receptivity or "hospitality" that involves both undergoing and outgiving, an active giving and opening of the self to others. To receive here means to "introduce", "admit", and "wel-

[1] *Du Refus à l'invocation*, p. 114.

77

come" into intimate participation in one's being, to be "at home" to others. *Chez soi* (at home) always involves a *soi* or *moi*, a personally qualified "inner space" into which others are welcomed.[1]

(*c*) For human existence is *personal*, the existence of a particular and unique self, and becoming a self requires opening-up to others, a co-presence or *I-thou* community. I become a personal self through taking other reality into my personal space or "living-room", in an act of "hospitality" that is also a "belonging"—to others, to the world, to God, and thus to my own being. I become a person through active and open confrontation of the basic situations of human existence and through disposability to and engagement in transcendent being.

I attain personal existence through action—not passively or automatically. The act and the person involve one another. Only the person can act. Action cannot be performed by the general "one" or "they" or by its functional particle, the individual isolated ego. It is of the essence of the person to *act, confront, envisage, assume responsibility, decide, commit himself.* "My act engages me."[2] There is an integral togetherness of me and my act, which is "incorporated in the totality of what I am". My whole life as integrated and consecrated, may be seen as a single act—a sacrament. The saint, the hero, and the artist demonstrate this through their lives and works.

The person strives to "envisage" his situation instead of merely undergoing it. He faces up to it. Confrontation involves appreciation and evaluation, an orientation in a particular direction. It involves

[1] *Du Refus à l'invocation*, p. 41 f.
[2] *Ibid.*, p. 142.

78

decision, personal commitment, self-engagement. I "expose" myself and "assume" responsibility, and thus make the act my own. I "assume" my act and thereby recognize myself in it. The nexus of the person with himself is realized in the act. Conversely, a man who is alienated from himself cannot act.

Our own time is haunted by the spectre of the anonymous, faceless, irresponsible "one" or "they" or "public"—the exact contrary of an "agent" or an "actor". The so-called "individual" is only a particle of the "one" or "they", a mere statistical element, a faceless sample—the object of merchandising surveys, public opinion polls, and mass communications. Indeed, the weight of the "one", of the accumulated and general, belongs to our condition, to our vulnerability as historical beings, and to our belonging to the realm of *it* as well as the realm of *thou*.

In a masterly interpretation entitled "The Ego and others",[1] Marcel distinguishes between the person and the ego in terms of being, disposability, and creativity. He seeks out the meaning of the statement "*C'est moi*" ("It is I"). The "I" here refers to the "me" and "mine" of "Look at me!", which means "Admire my this or that or the other"—my skills, talents, charms, possessions, that is, my property. It calls attention to myself as centre, excluding all others, and thus attaining self-satisfaction and self-confirmation. The person addressed is a mere means, a sounding-board to enable me to hear my own self-assertion amplified, necessary to me as an observer of my existence in the world. My "global presence", that is, my experience of being in the world, is given a particular

[1] *Homo Viator*, pp. 15–35 (English trans., pp. 13–28).

"accent" and localized as "me", and this is what I want you to notice. The anxiety of the void within and the feeling of self-encumbrance impel me to call out for confirmation from without and hence to encumber others with myself. This is the act of one who is a prisoner of his desires and feelings, cut off from his own reality, and hence is a poseur—seemingly before others, but actually before himself—in the idolatrous "cult of the ego". The social conditions most conducive to such egotism are those of competition—not only in economic but also in intellectual life, with its vicious stress on brilliant showings, on vying with one's fellows (who thus are degraded into rivals), and a popinjay "originality" ("Look at me!").

The person, however, as contrasted with the ego, is oriented in an absolutely opposite direction. Here the stress is not on "me" and "mine", but on the "gifts" and "vocation" that have been entrusted to me and need to be made good by me, to be realized and embodied in my life and work. Personal existence involves a direct confrontation of my situation, taking conditions as an opportunity and thus collaborating with my destiny, and an assumption of responsibility both before myself and before others "as a real being, participating in a particular, real society". In such personal, existential confrontation and responsibility I affirm the existence of the other person as himself—not merely as related to me, nor as an amplifier of my pretensions. Whereas the individual ego is blocked from contact with reality due to its self-fixation, anxiety, and closed-in-ness, the very mark of the person is disposability, the capacity to give oneself to what is present and thereby to bind oneself, to be-with.

This response is made to a "call" coming both from within and without. Artistic creation, for example, involves both the disposability of the artist to something beyond himself and his own decisive act. The creative process occurs in personal development as well as in art, for the person is bound up with the act whereby it creates itself, but is also dependent on an order which surpasses it and which in a sense it both discovers and invents in the act of becoming a person. Personal self-creation involves an openness to transcendent, suprapersonal reality in which the person is ultimately fulfilled. It involves self-consecration and self-sacrifice to something beyond oneself—a "creative fidelity" to being. In becoming persons, through our works and acts or indeed our whole lives, we become open to being. In becoming ourselves we go beyond ourselves; hence, we cannot be defined by the particular acts or expressions whereby we have become persons. Thus the person is not a completed entity, but a will, an aspiration to transcend present existence—*sursum*, not *sum*. Becoming a person requires incarnation, but the person can never be fixed in a particular incarnation; it "participates in the inexhaustible plenitude of being from which it emanates", that is, in a suprapersonal reality as its origin and end. However, incarnation in concrete acts and works is required for becoming a person. We must not get lost in abstractions. There is no hiding-place up there, warns Marcel, echoing Gustav Thibon—the way to heaven is to dig down deep where you are.

For Marcel, human existence is communal in two senses—with others and with oneself. In entering into community with others, we also establish community with ourselves. Marcel evokes the idea of a self-community as a "city-cell" of me and myself, a "dyadic" relation like that between an older and a younger brother—patient, loving, educative—a basic "dymorphism" (functional, not substantial), a duality of function of the one united person.[1]

In this sense, I can love myself, but self-love is not the egocentric obsession of the indisposable man—the egolatry which takes the self for a plenary and self-sufficient reality. It is rather charity toward oneself as potential being, as a seed or bud, a possible point of contact with the spiritual or divine. True self-love is not self-complacence or self-infatuation but a creative patience and lucidity that strive to bring forth the highest self-realization. Like every act of charity, it involves both distance and nearness—the capacity to see ourselves as we really are and yet to remain intimate with ourselves. When I love myself in this way it is not only myself I love, but all beings, just as the artist creates for all mankind, not for himself alone.

In this open, creative sense, there can be fidelity to the self. True self-fidelity is not conformity with a fixed "style" or habit of existence or constancy of opinion, a mere repetition or imitation of what I have done or thought or said before. Perpetual self-renewal and continual self-intimacy go together as they do in the artist who must respond freshly and anew to his inner call and continually transcend his past achievements if he is to be true to himself. In the state of self-alienation I become "profane" to the mystery of myself; I become a "deserter" and adopt the view of the outsider toward myself; I become ossified within my principles

[1] *Du Refus à l'invocation*, pp. 64–67.

and status and achievements. And as I become cut off from myself, I become cut off from others; the more intimate I am with myself the more I can be in real touch with my neighbour. What is this self with which I am intimate, this "presence" to which I am faithful? Marcel suggests it may be the divine spark of creativity within me, in any case a "mystery" which, just as that other self, is revealed only in love. There can be fidelity to oneself, then, as ontological "presence", but not to the finite ego with its claims, interests, and "having".[1] And in this sense, hope, too, can be exercised toward the self. Patience is practised toward the self as well as toward outer trials and other persons. Patience is an open attitude toward temporality, toward the possibility of change. Its keynote is "take your time". This means take your own time, your own rhythm, your own way. Don't rush it, don't distort things through fear and impatient haste as in an academic exam. Patience may be directed toward oneself (by the "elder" toward the "younger" self) as respect and consideration for one's unique rhythm, tone, and temper and as confidence in one's powers of growth. This is no passive non-intervention or complacent spectatorship in the face of inevitable development, but an active fostering of maturation, a "letting things be" which is a creative and transforming action. It is the opposite of despair about ourselves, of the attitude that we will never be any good, never do any better (as is often the attitude of parents toward children, teachers toward students, governors toward citizens). The relation of the hoper to his "trial" is analogous to that of the person to himself —a patient, relaxed governance and education, an

[1] *Homo Viator*, pp. 178–182 (English trans., pp. 129–132).

integration of the "trial" into oneself and its transformation within the creative process.[1]

This emphasis on self-relation and self-intention is paralleled by a stress on the "global", open character of the self. In a real relation between two beings, in the *I–thou* community, the distinction between "same" and "other" is transcended (or dimmed). The key line of Marcel's play *Quartet in F Sharp* is: "Thyself? Himself? Where does a personality begin? Each of us is prolonged in all that he evokes."[2] This "prolongation" occurs in the realm of "fertile indistinction", where beings communicate and so are. As I open myself up to the other he becomes *thou*, and in the presence of the *thou* I become unified, so that a dyad is now possible, instead of the triad of me-myself-and-he (where the other is a "third", an object of dialogue between me and myself). A mutual penetration of two beings, a primary living relation ensues upon which I cannot reflect without destroying it. But I naturally do so reflect and see the *thou* as a distinct "he" or "she": in our condition there is a rhythmic alternation between the concrete relation in which I am inseparably bound up with the *thou* and the reflection in which I separate myself from it and treat it as a distinct object. There is one exception to this natural intermittence: the relation to the Absolute *Thou* that can never become *it* for me.[3]

(*d*) The view that human existence intends *transcendence* is expressed in Marcel's evocative metaphor or ideogram "Homo Viator"—man the wayfarer, en route from existential brokenness to ontological fullness:

[1] *Homo Viator*, pp. 51–55 (English trans., pp. 38–41).
[2] *Le Quatuor en fa dièse*, p. 190.
[3] *Du Refus à l'invocation*, pp. 52–54.

Perhaps a stable earthly order can be established only if man retains an acute consciousness of what we may call his itinerant condition; that is, if he recalls perpetually that he has to beat a risky path across the uncertain blocks of a broken world which seems to be disappearing on all sides, toward a world more strongly established in being, and of which it is given to him to perceive here below only the changing and uncertain reflections. Does not everything occur as if that broken world turns implacably against him who claims to settle down there to the extent of building there a permanent dwelling? It is certainly not to be contested that the affirmation of that "beyond" carries a risk, the "noble risk" of which the ancient philosopher spoke, but the whole question is to know whether in refusing to run the risk one is not engaged in a road which, sooner or later, leads to perdition.[1]

By what right do we "extrapolate" from existence to transcendence? Hope gives us the right, says Marcel, prophetic hope, the "breath" of the soul. "It is precisely the soul that is a voyager, it is of the soul, and of it alone that it is supremely true to say that *being is to be en route.*"[2]

All our values, norms, and obligations acquire their transcendent character from being rooted in a real "beyond", and not from an abstract canon or a mental postulate. Value is always existentially incarnated and situated, but it points ultimately to transcendence, to the "beyond", to the Absolute *Thou.* Value sets upon life a "seal" that goes beyond time. It "exalts" us beyond our limits, beyond

[1] *Homo Viator*, p. 213 f. (English trans., p. 153 f.).
[2] *Ibid.*, p. 10, my italics (English trans., p. 11).

the situations which are the condition of human existence and creativity, and even beyond death where an "absolute sacrifice" is made.

Death for other men and for their good, for instance, is always death before the transcendent Other—even when it is an "atheist humanist" who sacrifices his life. Absolute fidelity to a being transcends and conquers death. "To love a being is to say, thou wilt never die," says Antoine in Marcel's play *Tomorrow's Dead*.[1] Anything else is betrayal—it is to give up one's beloved to death and take silence and invisibility for annihilation. For absolute fidelity, rooted in transcendence, the beloved dead is not an image or a memory or a shadow, but the "still existing" for me of what "no longer exists", a permanent, unfailing presence, with which I am in real relation.

Value is thus bound up with immortality and with eternal destiny. If death is ultimate, if it is the annihilation of being, then value becomes meaningless, reality becomes empty, and human communion is broken at its very core. Love, the "pledge and seed of immortality", involves "the recourse to absolute transcendence" and requires a going beyond all finite closedness and an opening up to that "universal communion" which alone can fully satisfy and which must depend on the Absolute *Thou*. Similarly, value, which may be doomed to futility and frustration in this "world of scandal and absurdity", seems to point to another world, of which it is the "mirror", where we may see our true destiny, a "beyond" to which our earthly existence opens the way or from which it excludes us.[2]

---

[1] *Trois Pièces*, p. 161.
[2] *Homo Viator*, pp. 200–213 (English trans., pp. 142–153).

VII

Religious Experience

From the beginning of his philosophical career, Marcel's main interest has been the interpretation of religious experience, that is, of the relation between man and ultimate reality. Jean Wahl recognized this in his pioneer essay on Marcel's thought in 1930—a long critical review of the *Metaphysical Journal*.[1] Marcel's early speculations on "participation", the *thou*-relation, and "trial", were followed in his later works by concrete, intuitive portrayals of fidelity, hope, "belonging", the familial bond, and other religious or quasi-religious aspects of human existence. Whereas the early work endeavours through rigorous meditation to present an abstract intellectual justification for the possibility of religious experience, the later work proceeds through an evocative portrayal of the basic situations of human existence, to indicate their essential religious intent—the direction of human existence toward primal reality. In his later period, Marcel understands religious experience as the experience of beings in the human condition—incarnate, in situation, and en route—living in contradiction, tension, and ambiguity, and seeking fulfilment in what goes beyond their present state. (Much of the interpretation of the

[1] "Le Journal Métaphysique de Gabriel Marcel", *Revue de métaphysique et de morale*, XXXVIII (1930), 75–112. Also included in Wahl's *Vers le concrèt* (Paris: Vrin, 1932), pp. 223–269.

"later" works was prepared by the meditations and explorations of the Second Part of the *Metaphysical Journal*, but is first fully expressed in *Being and Having*.)

Marcel has always seen religion as the relation of the human being in his wholeness to ultimate or transcendent reality. Putting his early and later views together, we may say that he sees this relation as an ontological "participation", an entering-in and opening-up to primal reality, involving "incarnation"—the ontological presence of one's own body and the world to one another—and dialogical or dyadic "communion" between an *I* and a *thou*. Hence he has rejected psychological theories of religious experience which try to reduce it to private states of intense "feeling", opposed to intellect and rationality and without an intention toward other reality. In his first play, *Grace*, the positivistic psychologist of religious experience, du Ryer, appears as an unpleasant and ridiculous character. For Marcel, religious experience is not merely a matter of private feelings, and "feeling" is of ontological, rather than merely psychological significance.

Marcel's "feeling" is first the immediate self-presence of one's own body and then the active opening to and entering into experienced reality— a creative, not a passive, "receptivity". It is through such active receptivity that we encounter other beings and the ultimate source of all beings. Feeling is a mode of "participation"—the supreme category in Marcel's interpretation of religious experience—and participation may be understood simply as being-with. In the human condition, feeling is a way of being-with, of actual conjunction and co-presence, and so are love and faith. But, for

88

Marcel, religious experience is not merely a private encounter between the soul and God; it always and pre-eminently involves being-with others, so that even in the act of solitary prayer the religious man participates in corporate communion. In the religious act we are not alone, either horizontally or vertically: that is to say, the religious act in its essential intention includes others and the Other.

Marcel's elucidation of the religious act is central in his interpretation of religious experience. He has interpreted the traditional religious virtues of faith, hope, and charity, the paradigmatic religious acts of prayer and sacrifice, the burden of sin and the striving for salvation in terms of the person's "disposability" to or "engagement" in ultimate or primal being. To render and evoke the meanings of religious acts and virtues he directs our attention first to the intentions and acts of ordinary experience, such as "fidelity", "witness", and "promise". If you want to understand religious faith, he suggests, look first at the ordinary human acts of putting-trust-in or being-faithful-to, of making a promise and bearing witness. You may not understand what it means to believe in God, but you may have some sense of what it means to trust a friend or to be faithful to your wife.

If you proceed in this way, says Marcel, you will see that the common everyday acts of hope, trust, or loyalty involve a fundamental disregard of the empirical conditions and relativities of human existence. They are, in their essential intent, unconditional, come-what-come-may, forever-and-aye, in-spite-of-everything. They are acts of and for the whole being (which at the moment of action is not fully and consciously known) and directed toward other beings; they are inter-ontological and involve an ultimate intention toward being itself. They are "creative" acts, which originate in the free initiative or response of the actor and which he may refuse to perform—a person is free to deny the ontological bond with other beings and thereby to being itself. But there is an ontological "exigence", an intense and deep-seated need for such a bond, in every one of us, and out of its frustration come despair and emptiness, a galling lack, impelling the victim to ontological union or self-negation.

Among the main elements of Marcel's theory of religious experience is his key category "participation", which denotes the interpenetration of beings, the togetherness or communion of realities, as opposed to the abstract, detached relation of subject and object—in thought or action. Participation is involved in the act of artistic creation or in aesthetic appreciation, in the love-relation between human persons, indeed in all the aspects of intimate human experience. It is not an abstract, conceptual affair of individuals and universals, as in ancient philosophical speculation, but the concrete "global" act of the whole human person; a concrete participation, involving pre-eminently "my body" and feeling, as well as intellect. Nor is it merely an objective reality, a brute metaphysical fact, with which personal will and impetus have nothing to do, as if we were mere filaments in the web of being. It involves an act of decision: one must decide to be-with or not to be-with, to enter into communion or to pull back into separation, to give credit, trust, and love, or to take the position of detachment from other beings and from being itself.

The affirmative choice requires the opening or making "available" of oneself, and the entering into other beings or into being itself; "disposability" and "engagement" are the receptive and active components of participation, respectively—being penetrated and penetrating. Hope and fidelity are Marcel's supreme examples of the participative-ontological act. In hope, "disposability" is at its absolute concentration, for no matter how incontrovertible the negativities of the empirical world (death, suffering, frustration, etc.), the soul remains open to the "absolute recourse", and the sufferer's ultimate reliance remains unshattered. (This absolute hope is fervently expressed in the Psalms.) Fidelity is the paradigm of "engagement", for it is the act of witnessing through one's own being and of remaining true to other beings, beyond all empirical limits, even beyond life, since it remains unaltered by death. "Disposability" and "engagement" are also involved in sacrifice and prayer, indeed in all the salient religious acts and situations. They also enter into the communion of an *I* with a *thou*—the essential mode of love between human persons and the model for the relation between man and God, which, in Marcel's view, is ultimately intended and involved in human love.

Marcel also develops in this context his concepts of "presence" and "invocation". The being I am with, which I adhere to, the *thou* which I intend and am bound to, must be present to me; I must make myself open to its presence and also be present to it. Again this is a "global" matter, not of a such-and-such, a finite something or someone that can be definitely and precisely described, conceived and imaged—not of an *it* or "object". It is the inter- or co-presence of two realities, of two beings, that we have to do with here, not the appraisal or handling of an external object by an autonomous, detached subject. This basic dichotomy of the two modes of relation with reality is stressed by Marcel all the way from the *Metaphysical Journal* to his later works, first as the distinction between existence and objectivity, then between mystery and problem, and finally between being and having.

The basic contrast is first presented as that between the sensible and the conceptual, for existence is sensible, and we participate in it through feeling; hence, this rich "sensible presence" is contrasted with the bare "mannequin-reality" of objective thought. Later, the contrast is made in terms of involvement and detachment, for being (the fulfilment of existence) is a "mystery" in which I am personally involved, something I am *in* and *with*, as opposed to something *before* me to be handled and solved—a "problem". And finally, being is distinguished from having, just as the "global" feeling which I am is distinguished from the communicable feelings that I have; and "my body" which I am, the basis of all having, is distinguished from all the body-objects which I try so avidly to possess.

In the total life of the spirit, these two modes of relation with reality are mutually involved and presuppose one another, but because of his philosophical struggle against idealism and positivism Marcel always stresses and pushes the primal mode, indicated by the words "existence", "mystery", and "being", as his favourite. It is an emphasis which points the way to the peculiar realm of religious experience. This, as we have seen, is interpreted in terms of a "dyadic" relation, a being-with, a dialogue involving a "call" and "response". The basic religious acts and situations—prayer, suffering ("trial"), hope, and faith—are interpreted in terms of the ontological dialogue. On our side of the dialogue is the self which prayer transforms and to which "trial" is sent, the self whose being is "at stake" and which is risked in the ultimate decisions of faith, the self which may be "saved" or "lost". On the other side is the "absolute recourse", the Absolute *Thou*, the transcendent Being toward which the person turns in humility, awe and reverence. We may approach the interpretation of this basic *religio* or communion through a consideration of the acts of religious worship, or an elucidation of the basic life-acts and -stances, or an interpretation of the familial bond.

Religious worship is for Marcel the paradigmatic act of being-with, of ontological communion, of opening-up and adherence to being. It is only in worship that any intimate knowledge of the Absolute *Thou* may be obtained; indeed, worship may be viewed as the starting-point for any philosophy of transcendence, and there may be a close analogy between worship and metaphysical vision or contemplation, with a common source in "wonder". But we may grasp the ultimate *religio* more easily in the basic acts of "engagement" and "disposability", as in the common acts of fidelity, witness, and promise, and in hope. Indeed, religious rites express the rhythm of fidelity, which is essentially being-with. And in the familial bond we may see the basic acts of fidelity and hope expressed and a turning toward the transcendent; for paternity is based on a "creative vow" which ultimately intends "the Holy" and is grounded in an eternal union of all in all. Paternity is a supreme act of piety, involving a co-working with creation and an embodiment of the sacred bond with reality through the bringing forth of new life. Indeed, human beings may be defined in terms of this creative relation to "the Holy". (See Marcel's essays "The Mystery of the Family" and "The Creative Vow as Essence of Fatherhood" in *Homo Viator*.)

But entirely apart from religious rites and sacraments and the piety expressed in familial relations, intimate human existence affords us both the pattern and the ground of religious consciousness, of the "dyadic" relation between the self and the Absolute. The shared experience of the human condition, of human "trial" and wayfaring, is common ground, is ours, "for us", and is deeply personal—"I exist", "I suffer", and "*I-thou*". Marcel indicated in the epigraph which he chose for the second part of the *Metaphysical Journal* that it is through considering intimate personal experience that we attain an awareness of infinite and ultimate reality—"It is private life that holds out the mirror to infinity; personal intercourse, and that alone, that ever hints at a personality beyond our daily vision."[1] The import of his interpretation of human existence is that to exist means to be influenceable by and directed toward otherness; it means being "en route" toward transcendent reality, toward the Absolute *Thou* that is addressed in prayer and heard in "trial". "I exist" connotes "I feel" (I am open to otherness), and then "I believe" (*in* Thee, or I am *with* Thee), which is the expression of pure "permeability" (Marcel's later and more precise denotation of "participation"). This is a matter of free decision, for I may choose to be "impermeable" and cut off from the Other. It is in the crises of life and in the presence of death that this experience and decision become most intense and crucial.

Death has a peculiar place in Marcel's thought as

[1] E. M. Forster, *Howard's End*.

part of the double-kingdom of our reality, indicating a "beyond" toward which our love and faith point, and which is the ultimate test and guarantor of love and value—the *thou*-relation always points beyond life. "There" resides the plentitude and perfection which is the fulfilment of human existence, toward which we ceaselessly journey, in our rôle of *homo viator*.

In sum, man's situation in the world, with its negativities and frustrations, is such that he must affirm or deny his being and his relation to ultimate being. This basic situation and these "trials" and this "exigence" are religious in nature; for they intend the basic bond with ultimate reality—and with the natural world, other beings, and oneself. Thus, faith not merely *intends* being or reality, but, ideally (trans-existentially), faith and being, that is, my faith and my being, are at one. Instead of saying, "Seeing is believing", Marcel would say, "Being is believing". Thus "belief", in this inter-ontological interpretation, means being-with, the belief *of us in Thee*. It is the ultimate affirmation of the reality "we are".

Marcel interprets all religious acts—prayer, rites, sacrifices, and so forth—as expressions of the basic intention to be—with the ultimate source and giver—in religious speech, "Thou"; in philosophical language, "Being". Such acts do not spring from a particular craving for a finite this-or-that, even for the boon of health or life itself; the intent of prayer, hope, and sacrifice go infinitely beyond the realm of *having* and its psychological symptom *desire*, to the kingdom of being and fulfilment. Praying, sacrificing, and hoping are humble acts of union-with ultimate reality, not petitions or pragmatic devices for the obtaining of finite

95

favours. In the religious act it is my being that is at stake, not my having.

Thus Marcel's interpretation of religious experience rests on two axes, ontological and anthropological: the participation in being and existential experience. It also depends on a peculiar method of understanding, which we may broadly designate "phenomenological" and which is discussed in the next chapter.

VIII

The Phenomenological Way

Very early in his career Marcel became concerned
with the problem of how to interpret basic realities
and experiences which he considered to be neither
logically demonstrable nor objectively describable.
The *Metaphysical Journal* records his first inquiries
into the understanding of religious faith, his ex-
ploration of sympathetic participation in distant
experiences and events, and his elucidation of the
thou-relation and of such basic religious experiences
as "trial" and prayer. At first it seemed to him that
such realities and experiences cannot be understood
by outside thought and observation: only the
"insider", the one who has had the experience, can
understand it. But his explorations of the basic religious experiences soon led him to introduce important qualifications of this negative position.
The "outsider", through participative sympathy,
may become an insider in a sense. The relation between two lovers, for instance, may be "rendered
sensible" indirectly through allusion; and the
"trial" of another man may be understood if we see
it as "ours" and regard him as "one of us", if
through the universalizing power of sympathy we
re-live and re-experience the life of our fellow
human being. Thus Marcel held that a specific
experience (such as the aesthetic or the religious)
can be "recognized" only from within—by the in-
siders, the lovers, the believers, etc.—but that others
may understand it through sympathetic evocation

and illumination. He continued to hold and develop this view all the way from the Second Part of the *Metaphysical Journal* to the formal public presentation of his position in the Gifford Lectures of 1950–51.

In the meantime, his development of an ontology of "we are", or being-with, and his appeal to our common participation in the human adventure had taken him a long way from the brusquely solipsist note of his early meditations that "the faith of others does not exist for me at all".[1] In such works as *Being and Having*, *Homo Viator*, and *From Refusal to Invocation*, he follows the way of indirect, concrete "approaches", of evocation and listening, via concrete metaphors and images, to feel out the meanings of the experience or concept under analysis.

This method may be characterized, broadly speaking, as "phenomenological". Marcel's method certainly places him with a school of present-day philosophers including Max Scheler, Martin Heidegger, Jean-Paul Sartre, and Maurice Merleau-Ponty whose theoretical foundations go back to Edmund Husserl, the father of "phenomenology". Marcel himself has occasionally acknowledged the likeness of tone and approach between his way and that of the German phenomenologists, and he sometimes uses characteristic Husserlian terms, such as "intentionality". Like Husserl, he emphasizes the philosopher as the "eternal beginner", calls for a return to "beginnings" or original experience, and uses the meditative method and evocative examples. As for Scheler, although there is no evidence of a seminal encounter between Marcel's mind and Scheler's thought, Marcel has been as notable as

[1] *Journal métaphysique*, p. 53 (English trans., p. 53).

Scheler for concrete phenomenological elucidations of religious acts. Although he was not influenced by Scheler in his formative period, Marcel did get to know Scheler's work, and apparently his use of the idea of "resentment" in the analysis of unbelief in *Being and Having* was influenced by Scheler's famous essay on the subject (on which Marcel wrote an unpublished critical review).

Broadly speaking, then, Marcel's method is "phenomenological", but there are basic contrasts between his metaphysical position and that of Husserl. As with his existential thought, Marcel worked out his phenomenological approach on his own hook, at his own pace, in his own particular way; if this is "phenomenology", it is Marcellian rather than Husserlian. Jean Héring, himself a French disciple of Husserl, sees Marcel as "an independent phenomenologist", who explored the method long before he encountered the work of Husserl and Scheler; and he ventures the opinion that even if the work of the German phenomenologists had remained unknown in France, a French phenomenology would have arisen independently, largely inspired by Marcel.[1]

Marcel's work has been not only independent but strikingly different. There could be no greater contrast than that between Husserl, the methodical German logician with his idea of philosophy as a rigorous science and with his search for "essences" completely purified of their existential embodiments, and the mature Marcel, with his idea of philosophy as originating in and continuously bearing on the basic situations of human existence.

[1] In Marvin Farber, ed., *Philosophical Thought in France and the United States* (Buffalo, N.Y.: University of Buffalo Publications in Philosophy, 1950), p. 74 f.

Marcel has expressed a repulsion for the neologisms and other abstruse procedures of the Husserlian school. He prefers ordinary language, everyday situations for examples, and a genial, warm, easy-going approach.

For an understanding of Marcel's method, we must go to his works. In his Gifford Lectures on *The Mystery of Being*, he tells us what he is trying to do and points out certain characteristics of his approach. He speaks of an "intermediary" type of thinking between the subjective and objective, the private and the common, that is, an understanding or appreciative consciousness, as in our experience of works of art. It is not commonly available, not for "no matter whom", because it requires a specific "exigence" for and intention toward a specific otherness; without such an inner demand and direction there can be no "recognition", and other reality can have no revelatory quality for us, can afford us no "illumination". But it is not merely private either, for it does bear—and this is essential—on something other. Our feelings, for instance, do have objective validity, in the sense that they refer to what is really "there"; but only the understanding mind can confer "reverberatory power", meaningfulness, on the facts, which thus become "radiant" and understandable. But again this is not mere subjectivism; it is becoming open to that which is really "there" in other reality, to what can become present to us, if we let it. It is to this that we must always get back, this original experience of other reality that is closed off by our secondary images and ideas, which become idols, or "simulacra", if we take them for the real thing.

The way to get to this real otherness is something like the way of the novelist who makes life "speak out" to us, or of the dramatist who makes characters and events present; it is an acting-out or bodying-forth, not a mere illustration of general truths. When I seek to know a flower, for instance, I am not satisfied by an analytical description of its class, genus, and species; I want to get at its singularity, its uniqueness, its essence, the flower that I actually experience, this present reality in which I participate. Similarly in our investigation of the religious act we seek its specific essence, not some abstract definition or a generalization of its observable, empirical characteristics. For example, in the case of the "sacrifice" of life, of "witness" or martyrdom, any fool can plainly see that this means physical death and annihilation, but this empirical, positivistic approach tells us nothing of the *essence* of "sacrifice"; indeed, as Marcel elucidates it, it gives us a totally false impression.

It must be stressed that the way of "understanding", just as consciousness itself, intends what is *other* than it. There is likeness, affinity, and involvement, but not sameness between the understanding mind and what it understands. The "faraway" is made close through understanding, a faraway which may be our own childhood or the antiquity of the race, the remote in time or the distant in space, other minds and other cultures.[1] Not *too* faraway, though, Marcel cautions, but perhaps midway between where I am now and the utterly exotic, for there must be an engagement or some possibility of engagement for there to be understanding.

Marcel carries this notion of intending the other still further. It is not merely that *thought* intends

[1] See Gerardus van der Leeuw, *Religion in Essence and Manifestation* (London: Allen and Unwin, 1938), p. 671 f.

otherness, but "my life" itself (which includes my consciousness) is essentially the *living* of something other; it is directed toward "transcendence", ultimate or absolute being or reality. But we see this basic "exigence" or "intention" first in common everyday relations with others, our companions of the daily round, or strangers met in sudden encounters—or in our community with our own past. In all of these relations we find the dimension of "depth" and the presence of "mystery", if we probe deep enough. The approach to all of these basic notions is the concrete one of taking what actually presents itself in experience, in certain cardinal situations of our daily life, and elucidating the "intention", the essential content and bearing of these acts (for instance, the cosmic piety embodied in family relations). This "phenomenological" approach is always made first, before entering into "hyper-phenomenological", or metaphysical, considerations.

We can see this especially clearly in the Gifford Lectures, where the approach to the "mystery of being" is made via the concrete consideration of my own existence, of "my life". The question "What am I?" precedes "What is being?" as providing *phenomenologically* the only possible starting-point. Thus we start with the primal "global" experience of our own existence, body, and feeling, and see this primary consciousness as an act of "exclamatory awareness", whose existence we cannot doubt. By way of concrete metaphors and examples we bring out the character of "participation" involved here, the note of "creative receptivity" about my feeling, and then make a *phenomenological* (not a metaphysical) distinction between two kinds of reality, or rather two types of entering into reality:

the participative/responsive and the detached/non-responsive. This is the same as the distinction between "presence" and "object" (or "mystery" and "problem"), two distinct types of turning toward reality. The act of worship, the peasant's relation to his soil or the artist's to his work, the magical "presentness" (immediacy) of poetry—these are Marcel's concrete images of the participative relation. He shows also how we may sense the mysterious power of "presence" in that sacred invulnerability protecting the weak who are in our power, for example, the guest, the wounded, the child, a sleeping person. Thus we look into the concrete acts and situations of our life, and through "reconnoitring", feeling our way, we come to "recognize" their essence and inner meaning.

For instance, we can explore the phenomenology of "tolerance". It is not merely a psychological matter of feeling or attitude, but lies somewhere on the "keyboard of experiences" between mere attitudes and a transcendent "spiritual dynamism", namely, charity. Tolerance intends the other as other, as he is, not reducing him to a tolerable form. It is a matter of positive "recognition" and "guarantee", a "mandate" in a realm where I have power, a personal act; not a mere negative "sufferance" or "endurance". It is exercised in a realm where I have power to be intolerant; hence, as an act of counter-intolerance, it is "reflective". I insist on granting freedom and respect to the other person who differs with me, as being one like myself, and taking him as he is in his own position. To the inevitable question about the universality and objectivity of truth, Marcel replies by admitting at once that tolerance emphasizes the subjective aspect of belief, as a mode of expression of human personality; but he insists that conversion to "true belief" is in the realm of freedom, love, and grace, and that the "true believer" must take the other as he is, *with his "heretical beliefs"*, with no holier-than-thou attitude and no idolatry of a tyrant-God. This open love of the other as he is, Marcel sees as a true witness to "the Holy". But now we are in the realm of "absolute religion", (of charity and grace) *beyond tolerance*, that is, above mere counter-intolerance. (In the case of political subversion, the civil authorities are necessarily *beneath* tolerance, and only countenance opinions which are not injurious to the health or life of the state.)

Marcel follows this analysis of tolerance in his handling of the ecumenical problem. He first distinguishes a truly catholic orthodoxy from mere conformism, as "open" universality versus "closed" fanaticism; hence, Catholicism essentially cannot act *against* any person or set up its own partial "claim" or counter-claim, but can work only in a spirit of charity and humility, bearing true witness to its faith. This is the only way in which the conversion of "heretics" can be catholically achieved, not in a spirit of "we" (*nous autres*) as against "you" or "they", of the good and wise as versus the bad and stupid. The act of witness is personal and humble, not a matter of pride in the superiority of one's arguments or of one's theological structure. Moreover, if Catholics adopt the phenomenological perspective and try to understand the other as such, as he is, in his place (and not theirs), they can see that "heresy" too is *lived* as a church and tradition by its adherents, and is not *experienced* by them as an incomplete sectarianism as against the "plenitude" of the Roman Catholic Church. If the latter takes such a stand it is being "particularist" and is itself making a sectarian "claim". Catholics must live and embody the truth they believe, says Marcel, and act with others in the work of justice and charity—this is a real bearing of witness.

Marcel even ventures to handle phenomeno-logically that old theological chestnut of the proof of the existence of God, that is, the question of human proof, not of divine existence. First Marcel gives us a phenomenological description of "proof": it is always toward others, made from some higher position which includes that of the one whom one is trying to convince, and it assumes some universal structures that can be agreed on, if brought to mutual "recognition". But we all recognize the notorious inefficacy of the traditional "proofs" of the existence of God with unbelievers, who do *not* proceed inevitably from the fact of *something* existing to that of *God* existing. The phenomenological way rejects the urge to dismiss the non-believer as being wilfully recalcitrant to cogent argument, and tries instead to understand him with a sympathy which helps believers to put themselves in his place and see his unbelief as *he* sees it. It may be that he simply decides not to follow the theistic line of argument because he does not want to go where it leads, since it conflicts with his basic experience or his urge to independence; either he cannot honestly admit the presence of a Supreme Good in the world, as he has experienced it, or he chooses him-self as that Good, and so can allow nothing to exist above him. A basic agreement on values is neces-sary for any successful proof; but this is missing, where no transcendent Good is admitted. More-over, the concrete situation of dislocation in a "broken world" must be taken into account as obstacle (or springboard) to belief. It is only as himself being in this situation, and out of his own inadequacy, out of the unbelief in his own heart, that the believer is able to approach the unbeliever, realizing that the other is bereft of the gift that has been given him, and on this common ground of a "broken world" convincing the other through witness and the "radiation" of faith, rather than by words and logic.[1]

If we turn back to the early beginnings of Marcel's thought in the *Metaphysical Journal*,[2] we find there the description and elucidation of a faculty which may throw some light on Marcel's method in his later works. We may call this faculty "divination". Marcel elucidates it in terms of his cardinal doctrine of "participation". According to this, "vision" of what is remote in space or time is basically a being-with, and what is "seen" or "heard" comes as response to our "call", through our emotional involvement, "concern", or "interest". The intent of spiritual experience is knowable only through a participative love and sympathy, through a reliving or "trans-living" (a personal living-through, rather than an objective trans-mission). "Recognition" of what is "there", beyond our limits and our life, comes only through the interested person, who in his re-experiencing and re-feeling, comes to be at one (though not identical) with what he experiences or feels. Hence

[1] The above examples have been chosen from these essays in *Du Refus à l'invocation*: "L'Orthodoxie contre les Conformismes", "En marge de l'Œcuménisme", "Phénoménologie et dialectique de la Tolérance", "Méditation sur l'idée de preuve de l'existence de Dieu".

[2] See esp. pp. 129 f., 134 f., 162–175, 188–195, 233–253 (English trans., 129 f., 134 f., 162–174, 192–198, 240–261).

"the faith of others" does exist for me insofar as the other's belief *in* becomes for me belief *with*, through my sympathetic participation. This requires a re-forming and an opening of the self. The "mystery" of love and faith is thus knowable via participation, or, indeed, knowing is participation.

Marcel's portrayal and interpretation of the "seer" and the power of "vision" in the *Metaphysical Journal* provides a striking example of this process. It points to the possibility of the recapture of the past through actual participation in other-reality, proceeding from the objective "document" or thing to a "trans-living" of the whole context, so that via a sudden opening afforded by suggestion, the dead past becomes alive and present again. The seer's vision requires a prior "purification", an emptying-out and opening-up, as well as a recol-lection, of the mind that would see into the past or view a distant scene or event; an ascetic preparation that perhaps does not come to mind at once with regard to other methods of knowing, but is cer-tainly involved in any rigorous knowledge, even the narrowest kind, and enters in whenever vision and contemplation are essentially required.

This method puts an enormous burden on the probity and sincerity of its practitioner, but still more it requires a concentration on and an open-ness to the freshness and suggestion of original ex-perience which will hardly be widespread in academic circles, since to possess such qualities one must become as a child again, or have something of the poet and dreamer, of the new-maker and see-er about him. This method requires that every man be the judge of the truth of his findings, just as the artist knows when his painting is right and he alone may be able to sense when and why this little smudge of red must be put there. Such instantaneous insight and affirmation is similar to what the phenomenologists call "evidence". There is nothing really extraordinary about this; we all have such intuitions and acknowledge the sanction of such "evidence" in our deeply intimate every-day life.

Moreover, according to Marcel, there is a universal epistemological basis for the interpretation of religious and existential experience in our common human adventure, our undergoing of the basic human condition and situation, our fraternal wayfaring and destiny. He continually starts from here and continually appeals to our common case, to the "we are", our mutual being-with. He has seen himself as, like Jaspers, making "calls" to other wayfarers, waiting and hoping for their response, taking this common feeling to indicate that this is the true way into reality. Thus he puts his trust in the open intuition of personal existence, deeply experienced and understood, as leading to a commonly grasped reality. The phenomenological way is for Marcel the gateway to the ontological realm.

IX

L'Envoi

Half a century ago Marcel began his prophetic protest against "official" philosophy and the idolatry of "verification". He fought against the dogma that only what can be related to the so-called "normal" and "universal" conditions of experience may be regarded as real and meaningful. This criterion effectively denied existence to the philosophical consciousness of whole realms of experience, both below and above the "verifiable". Some of the highest and deepest, as well as the most primal, experiences of human beings were thereby ruled out or reduced and falsified to fit into the rubrics of an accepted "normality" and "verifiability". A philosophy thus restricted, Marcel was convinced, whatever its merits in certain specialized realms of inquiry, has nothing essentially to do with living, incarnate man in his concrete situation in the world, with his vocation to become himself and to connect with reality. The genuine philosopher is called upon to discover or recognize truth through the patient and sensitive fathoming of his own deepest personal experience, and thereby to arrive at the common ground of truth—aided by the open dialogue, the interchange of "calls" and "responses" with his fellow men.

Against the "official" mutilation and falsification of experienced reality, Marcel, therefore, allied himself with the nineteenth century rebels, such as Schopenhauer, Kierkegaard, and Nietzsche, who, through their example as well as their words, called on the philosopher to give up the pose of being a philosopher "as such", a mere *Fachmensch* or specialist, and to acknowledge instead that he is the particular person he is, with his particular experience, and to speak from his particular situation. Any true grasp of philosophical problems requires personal exigence and struggle; for philosophy in this large, human sense cannot be objectively appropriated or transmitted. The philosopher must philosophize here and now, naked and unarmoured, constantly open and vulnerable to the "shock" of reality, always astonished by its "bite", continually its "prey", rather than comfortably situated in some traditional, conventional, or currently fashionable safety-island above the human condition.

"Philosophy," Marcel has said, "is an uplifting of experience, not its castration."[1] It was to this uplifting of experience and against its castration that he directed his philosophical quest. He summoned up the image of a "metaphysical Atlantis", submerged below the surface of conventional and academic consciousness, which it is the task of the philosopher to touch upon at its rare and illuminable "outcroppings" and thereby to restore the lost wholeness of human reality, with its roots in bodily existence and its intention toward being.[2] Hence Marcel's persistent attempt, beginning with the meditations in the *Metaphysical Journal*, to illuminate areas of human experience that are the most difficult and refractory to rational analysis and usually the most neglected by conventional philosophy.

[1] *Du Refus à l'invocation*, p. 109.
[2] See *ibid.*, p. 124.

Marcel's remarkable accomplishment in restoring to us our lost Atlantis, in revivifying the comatose and darkened sectors of our experience through the investigation and reclaiming of his own, has been narrated in the preceding chapters. This work of prophetic protest and creative elucidation originated in a particular historical hour and is marked in many of its details and concerns by the intellectual situation in which Marcel found himself. That situation has changed in many respects. The historical and even the psychological study of religion can no longer be justly represented by the positivistic caricature which Marcel drew in the *Metaphysical Journal* and his play *Grace*. Human and social studies have displayed an increasing sensitivity, depth, and openness to the actual life of concrete human beings. Existential and phenomenological philosophies dominate the scene in continental Europe and have penetrated theological faculties and intellectual circles even in Britain and the United States.

Nevertheless, we still have to struggle, like Marcel, against new officialdoms and idolatries that have arisen or threaten to arise. The hard won insights and intuitions which he attained through a painful and tortuous personal struggle may now have become the catchwords of a new "official" philosophy, a new scholasticism *à la mode*. A "dialogistics" may be envisaged which is more likely to be the barrier than the road to true dialogue and an understanding of dialogue; and a systematic "existology" which is more likely to lead to a new ossification and dogmatics, to a new "scholarization", than to personal existence and concrete awareness. Besides, we of the English-speaking world face as bleak a philosophical prospect as ever confronted Marcel when he began his quest: the idol of "verification" in its positivistic form is still very much with us, and the analysis of language, a game of small gains and little risk, dominates the philosophical scene, almost to the exclusion of the fathoming and illumination of concrete human existence. A new restrictive covenant seems to be in the making, limiting what is meaningful and communicable in human experience to what is so validated by the protagonists of the dominant school of philosophy—at the moment —in British and American universities. Whenever and wherever such restrictive covenants exist, belying our actual existence and experience and stifling our intellectual awareness and expression, Marcel's creative protest becomes relevant and must be renewed; he presents us with a persistent witness, example, and challenge.

And, it should be stressed, this new restrictive covenant is not only vicious and intolerable as far as our individual existence and consciousness is concerned, but is immeasurably more so as it cuts us off from communication with the common existence of mankind, with those who have gone before us and those who will come after us—with the ancients and the primitives, and, assuming that man is to remain man, with the man of the future too. The patrimony "recuperated" by Marcel is potentially present in each of us, connecting us with the past and the future by opening us to the depths of our own existence. Such a restoration and liberation serves to rescue us from the solipsism of the present socio-historical moment and its intellectual fashions.

However, as Marcel has noted, traditional rationalism, Stoicism, Spinozism and Thomism also mutilate and falsify our experience of reality. These traditional philosophical movements, which often deny our concrete, historical, incarnate, personal existence even more effectively and completely than modern empiricism and positivism, have displayed enduring strength, as witnessed by their periodic revivals in modern times. Although these traditional ways of thought started originally in some authentic and concrete response to reality, they have degenerated through centuries of parrot-philosophizing into scholastic apparatuses, spiritless commentaries and the various "isms" and neo-"isms" which shut off rather than spread the original light.

As against this, Marcel offers the way of "concrete philosophy", which concentrates solely on the transmutation, deepening, and illumination of the philosopher's own situation and experience. Such a philosophy, however, is not thereby "subjectivist" either in its intention or its result. The quest and the experience in this case have been Marcel's, and his way has often been a lonely as well as a tortuous one; but he has never been interested merely in singing the song of himself, in some limited, egotistic, solipsist sense. As Paul Ricoeur has pointed out, the *Metaphysical Journal* is not a *journal intime*, a private diary that merely retails the acts and thoughts and feelings of Gabriel Marcel, but an investigation of the human condition, in which he shares with all men an inquiry open to all of us.

Marcel has seen himself as making "calls" through his published meditations and expectantly awaiting "responses", relying on our community of condition and the common bond of intersubjectivity for a free and uncoerced agreement. (A

Hume today, he once remarked, would call his work *A Treatise on the Human Condition*.) An appeal to the common element in our intuitions and experiences is as important in his thought as is the constant stress on specific disposition and receptivity; for, indeed, the latter, though not for "anyone"—for the anonymous, untouched, external spectator-in-general—are open to all men. Like Socrates in Plato's *Gorgias*, Marcel has looked to a community of feelings to assure a communication of impressions and experience between men. That is one of the reasons why he has preferred to be known as a "neo-Socratic" or a "Christian Socratic" rather than as an existentialist, finding an affinity with Socrates' interrogative, dialogical stance, his constant address to a concrete *thou*, and his depreciation of "any kind of physics" as irrelevant to ultimate human concerns.[1]

The works of this unpretentious philosopher of personal experience are expressed for the most part in fragmentary meditations and essays ("attempts"), but they cover a lot of ground and deal with many of the areas that have long been the objects of philosophical inquiry. Careful investigators will find in Marcel's works an ethics, an aesthetics, an epistemology and a social philosophy, as well as a philosophy of religion and a doctrine of personal existence. Marcel has no natural philosophy in the traditional sense, nor does modern scientific knowledge play an important role in his thought. He has no philosophy *about nature*, about the physical cosmos, about the structure of the universe; but he does have something significant to say *about man's relation to nature*. Some of the most notable essays in *Homo Viator* are concerned with

[1] See Preface to *Metaphysical Journal*, p. xiii.

the bond between man and the natural world, with the cosmic piety which Marcel considers essential for a spiritually whole and healthy human existence, as "the only true *vinculum* which can bind men together".[1] Marcel has resolutely opposed any eschatalogical, pessimistic form of Christianity, or any mystical withdrawal which "unhallows" the natural world and the lived reality of human existence and thus cuts man off from the natural basis of ethics and religion. This stress distinguishes Marcel's thought from the type of existentialist philosophy which disregards or opposes the natural world or sees it in its inmost core as *Dreck*. We should also recall that Marcel has offered a phenomenological and existential interpretation of the role of the body in human life through his elucidation of man as an incarnate being and a being in situation.

This constant affirmation of the positive value and meaning of the natural world tends to dispel in part the apprehensions arising from the Gnostic overtones of certain statements in his works, which point yearningly toward the transcendence in a perfect "beyond" of an evil and cracked world order. Perhaps the ghost of Gnosticism with its two-worlds doctrine lurks temptingly at the shoulder of every serious Christian thinker. Alive to these implications, Marcel has declared that he espouses an ethical, not a metaphysical, dualism, a practical rather than a theoretical Manicheism.[2] His "beyond", he asserts, is not literally suprater-restial, not some other place, but an unknown and higher dimension of reality, attainable in and through human experience and existence. In an

[1] *Homo Viator*, p. 226 (English trans., p. 162).
[2] *Les Hommes contre l'humain*, p. 94 (English trans. p. 92 f.).

illuminating discussion of his plays, entitled "The Drama of the Soul in Exile", Marcel traces the peculiar union of the immediate and the transcendental in his thought and categorically rejects any implication of Platonic dualism. "For me, the soul in exile is the soul which has become a stranger to itself, which can no longer understand itself, which has lost its way, . . ." in contrast with the soul of "Platonists throughout the ages . . . the soul, sunk after some scarcely imaginable spiritual disaster, in the darkness of the world of sense and aspiring to expand once more in some intelligible empyrean".[1]

Marcel has also affirmed the positive value of reason, that is, of objective rational thought. However, his evaluation of "objectivity" and "primary reflection" and his interpretation of their relation to "participation" and "secondary reflection" are often obscure, eliciting objections from such sympathetic and perceptive interpeters of his thought as Troisfontaines and Ricoeur. His discussion of the realm of objectivity, *it*, and the verifiable in the early period when he hewed out the main roads of his thought is markedly pejorative in tone. In his polemic against absolute idealism and empirical positivism, Marcel apparently became so completely absorbed in fighting against the unwholesome excesses and distortions of objectivity and in restoring the realm of *thou* and the unverifiable, that he paid little attention to the proper and wholesome role of rational analysis and abstractions in human thought, and the special applications of technical reason in human life. Not only a questionable denigration of natural human powers is thereby suggested, but a permanent split

[1] *Three Plays*, p. 16.

seems to be implied in the human wholeness which it has been Marcel's particular aim to restore.

Despite passing remarks acknowledging the validity and role of objective knowledge and detached analysis, Marcel's early, formative work is certainly vulnerable to such criticisms. Unlike a Whitehead or a Jaspers, Marcel has not been personally involved in the sciences of our time (save perhaps for his early interest in psychology) and has not followed attentively the new uses and developments of rational analysis and objectivity. (Ricoeur suggests that even in philosophy Marcel has not taken cognizance of the new epistemological developments, such as the Husserlian, beyond the idealist and positivist forms of objectivity.)

Aware of these criticisms, Marcel has attempted in his later years to clarify and defend his position in regard to abstractions and techniques (especially in *Men Against Humanity*, *The Decline of Wisdom*, and the Preface to Troisfontaine's monumental presentation of his thought). Marcel's defence, in brief, is that he does affirm the positive role and value of rational analysis in the apprehension of reality, as well as the proper technical application of reason to fulfil the ends of human life. What he opposes, he says, is not abstraction, but "the spirit of abstraction" which sets up abstractions in place of the concrete reality they are designed to illuminate and which imprisons us at the stage of primary, separative analysis and prevents us from going on to the stage of secondary, integrative reflection and a higher and richer level of concrete reality. Marcel's emphasis, we see, is still on the restoration of integral reality, on therapy, while the connection or collaboration between the two modes or levels, the theory, remains obscure and elusive. In the

Preface to Troisfontaines, for instance, Marcel sees the necessity for finding and illuminating the connection between the body/object and the body/self, between the technically manipulable and the charismatically affectable perspectives of the body, but he leaves the connection open and yet to be disclosed. Marcel has no interest in systematically coordinating the various levels of reality or modes of awareness, in order to attain a synoptic vision of the whole. He has never considered this to be the work that he was called upon to do.

More important than the achievement or non-achievement of a systematic metaphysics or epistemology, however, in terms of Marcel's own thought, is the meaning and value of rational analysis and abstractions in the spiritual life of the concrete inquirer. In the Preface to Troisfontaines, the empirical scientist is portrayed as engaged with only a part of his being, as against the true philosopher who is engaged with his whole being. Granted that the abstractive and analytical is a special function of the human spirit, and that the philosopher in Marcel's sense works concretely and integrally, with all his parts, this seems to be a plausible statement. Yet, again in terms of Marcel's own thought, it raises certain significant questions. Can abstract thought too be the medium, the form of expression, of an existentially rooted drive toward ontological participation? Is not something like this the basic intention of the great philosophers of the past—of an Aristotle and Aquinas, and also of a Plato and a Descartes? Can what Marcel calls "the whole being" be committed and involved in the life-vocation of abstract thought?

A similar line of questioning was indicated

many years ago by Franz Rosenzweig, another religious existentialist and concrete philosopher, when he conceded that the rarified, abstract arguments for God's existence were orginally "honest knowledge", rooted in an actual human situation and of concern to concrete men. Granted that the abstractions are remote from the living God, says Rosenzweig, it is not the "nearness" or "remoteness" that is essential, but the intention and the concern (the mutual concern between man and God), for,

> ... even at a very great distance, the burning gaze of God and man fuse in such a way that the coldest abstractions grow warm in the mouth of Maimonides or Hermann Cohen—warmer than all our agonized drivel . . . What matters is that, near or remote, whatever is uttered is uttered before God, with the "Thou". . . that never turns away.[1]

Marcel has of course been aware that merely crying, "Existence! Existence!" will not bring us into the kingdom of human reality (many of his plays reveal the dangerous pitfalls of such spiritual inauthenticity and pretentiousness), and he has acknowledged the ontological intention and concrete rootedness of the great abstract thinkers of the past (although again he has not spelled this out or emphasized it at any length). He has also noted the personal role of the scientist in research, maintaining that "the person of the scientist with all his good and bad powers" is engaged in his work, and that this has a marked "personal and

[1] *Franz Rosenzweig: His Life and Thought.* Presented by Nahum N. Glatzer. New York: Schocken Books (Farrar, Strauss, and Young), 1953, p. 280 f.

dramatic" quality, involving not merely the impersonal march of science, but "the realization of an individual destiny".[1]

But here again it is not empirical science or scientific scholarship or the famous "laboratory experiment" that is the basis of Marcel's thought—but intimate personal experience, to which he appeals as common ground, referent, and "proof". He calls to each individual person, scientist or not, to look into himself and his life, to "taste", as the Psalmist says, and thereby realize his existence and his destiny. Through the way of friendly persuasion and concrete evocation, the way of call and response, he points to the common universal ground of integral personal experience, the matrix from which all else that is human is derived, the constant point of origin and return.

[1] *Du Refus a l'invocation*, p. 45 f.

Appendix

Hegel's works, especially the *Phenomenology of Mind* and the *Logic*, were important in shaping Marcel's early thought; late in life he still expressed admiration for Hegel, praising in particular the latter's "preservation of the primacy of the concrete". Quite early he was drawn to Schelling, with his idea of a higher empiricism, of a new immediacy and concreteness beyond the stage of analytical reflection; Marcel's thesis for his diploma in higher studies was a comparison between Coleridge's metaphysical ideas and Schelling's philosophy. At the Sorbonne he encountered Léon Brunschwig, the redoubtable leader of French idealism and a determined exponent of the transcendence of the ideal, of the priority of the abstract "spiritual" over the concrete and of reason over faith; the clash with Brunschwig's thought was apparently a vital factor in the development of Marcel's.

The Anglo-American idealists—first Bradley and Bosanquet, then Royce and Hocking—were important influences on Marcel's thought. Bradley and Royce in particular served him both as allies and adversaries in the development of his thought "toward the concrete", toward the intersubjective communion of unique individualities, toward the immediate relation with transcendent reality. He used and developed major ideas of theirs (such as "global feeling", "triadism", "intersubjectivity", and "loyalty") and determinedly rejected others (such as the "integration" of appearances or individuals into Reality or the Absolute, and the predominance of ideal thought over concrete reality), as they fitted in or conflicted with the basic direction of his own thought. From Hocking he got the idea of "participation" as a real relation of individual beings to ultimate being through faith and love; he credits Hocking with having set him on the road to a "new realism".

Among thinkers at the turn of the century, Bergson was undoubtedly the closest to Marcel in his attitude and emphases, and played an important role in Marcel's development. Bergson's critique of idealism, his espousal of the primacy of the concrete over the abstract, and his attack on intellectualism and systematization in favour of the spontaneous life of thought struck a responsive chord in Marcel. Also Bergson's notion that intuition is more analogous with touch than with vision fitted in with Marcel's groping toward a non-optical interpretation of thought. However, Marcel rejected Bergson's dichotomy between intelligence and intuition, preferring instead a distinction *in* thought between "thinking thought" (thought in the making) and "thought thought" (the finished products of thinking). In his first published article Marcel insisted that intuition has meaning and value only if it is undergirded by a "dialectic" into which it has previously been inserted; he compared intuition with an act of faith whose content is made explicit through a "practical dialectic of participation" oriented toward "He Who Is". Marcel also rejected Bergson's notion of a "privileged thought" which might grasp "pure duration", as being opposed to the conditions of human existence; and he was averse to the notion of the *élan vital* and the fusion of subject and object, in which the substantial, intimate reality of the human person is lost.

Etienne Gilson has seen Marcel as an independent disciple of Bergson, who, starting from the same initial "realist" principle of the primacy of concrete reality over abstract thought, carried it further than his master dared, into a new philosophy of being—which, however, may be most easily approached by way of Bergsonism. Marcel has expressed unreserved gratitude toward Bergson, crediting him with providing the example without which he himself would probably never have had "either the courage or the capacity" to undertake his own philosophical quest. Marcel acknowledged his indebtedness to Bergson and Hocking in the dedication to the *Journal métaphysique* (inexplicably omitted from the English translation):

> To Mr. Henri BERGSON,
> To Mr. W. E. HOCKING,
> in expression of my deep gratitude

These are the major influences on the formation of Marcel's thought—from Hegel to Hocking. After he reached his philosophical maturity, he had many fruitful encounters and clashes with thinkers of his own generation—particularly with Karl Jaspers and Martin Heidegger.

Biographical Note

Gabriel Marcel was born in Paris, December 7, 1889. His father was a state counsellor, French minister to Sweden, and director of the Beaux-Arts, Bibliothèque nationale, and Musées nationaux. Marcel's mother died when he was four, and he was brought up by her sister, who became his father's second wife and played an important role in the development of his mind and character. He was of Jewish descent on his mother's side. Although a brilliant student as a boy, he loathed the impersonal, objectivist education to which he was subjected and the constant parental pressure to get top grades; in later life he remembered his school days with horror. An only child and a lonely child, he found creative enjoyment and companionship in the conversations he invented with imaginary characters who peopled the dramas that he began writing at an early age. Foreign travel fulfilled an inner need to become intimate with the strange and faraway, beginning with a memorable sojourn in Sweden at the age of eight when he accompanied his father on his mission to Stockholm. Marcel was educated at the lycée Carnot and the Sorbonne in Paris, attaining his *Agrégation de philosophie* in 1910, but never completing his doctoral thesis (on the necessary conditions for the intelligibility of religious thought). He taught philosophy at various lycées, but, except for the period 1915–22, he held teaching posts only at rare intervals and pursued his career as a free-lance intellectual. He worked as a reader for two

Paris publishers, Plon and Grasset, and was the editor of Plon's *Feux Croisés* series (a collection of translations of works by notable contemporary foreign writers) from 1927. In addition to his creative work in philosophy and drama, he was a prolific author of literary and dramatic criticism from the early 1920s. Marcel won the Grand Prix de Littérature de l'Académie Française in 1948, the Goethe Prize in 1956, the Grand Prix National des Lettres in 1958, the German Booksellers' Peace Prize in 1964, and the Erasmus Prize in 1969. He was Gifford Lecturer at Aberdeen in 1949–50 and William James Lecturer at Harvard University in 1961. A member of the Institut de France and of the Académie des Sciences Morales et Politiques, an officer of the Légion d'Honneur, a commander of the Ordre des Arts et des Lettres and of the Ordre des Palmes Académiques, he received the honor of Grand Croix in the Ordre National du Mérite in 1972. Marcel died in Paris, October 8, 1973.

The Association Internationale "Présence de Gabriel Marcel," 9, Avenue Franklin Roosevelt, 75008, Paris, France, is a center for information and discussion about Marcel's life and work.

MARCEL'S WORKS

Philosophy

Journal métaphysique. Paris: Gallimard, 1927. (*Metaphysical Journal.* London: Rockliff, 1952; Chicago: Regnery, 1952.)

Être et avoir. Paris: Aubier, 1935. (*Being and Having.* Westminster: Dacre, 1949; Boston: Beacon, 1951.)

Du Refus à l'invocation. Paris: Gallimard, 1940. Republished as *Essai de philosophie concrète.* Paris: Gallimard, 1967. (*Creative Fidelity.* New York: Farrar, Straus & Giroux, 1964.)

Homo Viator: Prolégomènes à une métaphysique de l'espérance. Paris: Aubier, 1945. (*Homo Viator: Introduction to a Metaphysic of Hope.* London: Gollancz, 1951; Chicago: Regnery, 1952.)

La Métaphysique de Royce. Paris: Aubier, 1945. (*Royce's Metaphysics.* Chicago: Regnery, 1956.)

"Regard en arrière," in *Existentialisme chrétien: Gabriel Marcel,* by Etienne Gilson, *et al.* Paris: Plon, 1947. ("*An Essay in Autobiography,*" in *The Philosophy of Existence.*)

The Philosophy of Existence. London: Harvill, 1948; New York: Philosophical Library, 1949. Republished as *The Philosophy of Existentialism.* New York: Citadel, 1956.

Positions et approches concrètes du mystère ontologique. Louvain: Nauwelaerts and Paris: Vrin, 1949. ("On the Ontological Mystery," in *The Philosophy of Existence.*)

Le Mystère de l'être. Tome I: *Réflexion et mystère;* Tome II: *Foi et realité.* Paris: Aubier, 1951. (*The Mystery of Being.* Vol. I: *Reflection and Mystery;* Vol. II: *Faith and Reality.* London: Harvill, 1950–51; Chicago: Regnery, 1951–52.)

Les Hommes contre l'humain. Paris: La Colombe, 1951. (*Men Against Humanity.* London: Harvill, 1952. *Man Against Mass-Society.* Chicago: Regnery, 1952.)

Le Déclin de la sagesse. Paris: Plon, 1954. (*The Decline of Wisdom.* New York: Philosophical Library, 1955.)

L'Homme problématique. Paris: Aubier, 1955. (*Problematic Man.* New York: Herder & Herder, 1967.)

The Influence of Psychic Phenomena on My Philosophy. London: Society for Psychical Research, 1956.

Présence et immortalité. Paris: Flammarion, 1959. (*Presence and Immortality.* Pittsburgh: Duquesne U.P., 1967.)

Fragments philosophiques, 1909–1914. Louvain: Nauwelaerts, 1961. (*Philosophical Fragments: 1909–1914;* and *The Philosopher and Peace.* Notre Dame: University of Notre Dame Press, 1965.)

La Dignité humaine et ses assises existentielles. Paris: Aubier, 1964. (*The Existential Background of Human Dignity.* Cambridge: Harvard University Press, 1963.)

Paix sur la terre. Paris: Aubier, 1965.

Searchings. New York: Newman, 1967.

Pour une sagesse tragique et son au-delà. Paris: Plon, 1968. (*Tragic Wisdom and Beyond, Including Conversations between Paul Ricoeur and Gabriel Marcel.* Evanston: Northwestern University Press, 1973.)

Entretiens Paul Ricoeur, Gabriel Marcel. Paris: Aubier, 1968. (*Conversations between Paul Ricoeur and Gabriel Marcel,* in *Tragic Wisdom and Beyond.*)

En chemin, vers quel éveil? Paris: Gallimard, 1971.

Coleridge et Schelling. Paris: Aubier, 1971.

Entretiens autour de Gabriel Marcel. Neuchâtel: La Baconnière, 1976.

Gabriel Marcel interrogé par Pierre Boutang. Paris: Place, 1977.

Drama and Criticism

Le Seuil invisible (*La Grâce, Le Palais de sable*). Paris: Grasset, 1914.

Le Coeur des autres. Paris: Grasset, 1921.

L'Iconoclaste. Paris: Stock, 1923.

Un Homme de Dieu. Paris: Grasset, 1925; La Table Ronde, 1950. (*A Man of God,* in *Three Plays.*)

Le Quatuor en fa dièse. Paris: Plon, 1925.

Trois Pièces (*Le Regard neuf, La Mort de demain, La Chapelle ardente*). Paris: Plon, 1931.

Le Monde cassé. Paris: Desclée de Brouwer, 1933. (With postface: "Positions et approches concrètes du mystère ontologique.")

Le Dard. Paris. Plon, 1936.

Le Fanal. Paris: Stock, 1936. (*The Lantern,* in *Cross Currents,* Vol. 8, No. 2, Spring 1958.)

Le Chemin de crête. Paris: Grasset, 1936. (*Ariadne,* in *Three Plays.*)

La Soif. Paris: Desclée de Brouwer, 1938. (Republished as *Les Coeurs avides*. Paris: La Table Ronde, 1952.)

L'Horizon. Paris: Aux Étudiants de France, 1945.

Théâtre comique (*Colombyre ou le Brasier de la paix, Le Double expertise, Les Points sur les I, Le Divertissement posthume*). Paris: Albin Michel, 1947.

Vers un autre royaume (*L'Emissaire, Le Signe de la Croix*). Paris: Plon, 1949.

La Fin des temps. Paris: *Réalités*, No. 56 (1950).

La Chapelle ardente. Paris: La Table Ronde, 1950. (*The Funeral Pyre*, in *Three Plays*.)

Rome n'est plus dans Rome. Paris: La Table Ronde, 1951; Les Oeuvres Libres, No. 63 (1951).

Three Plays (*A Man of God, Ariadne, The Funeral Pyre*). London: Secker & Warburg, 1952; New York: Hill & Wang, 1958. (With preface: "The Drama of the Soul in Exile.")

Mon temps n'est pas le vôtre. Paris: Plon, 1955.

Croissez et multipliez. Paris: Plon, 1955.

La Dimension Florestan. Paris: Plon, 1958. (With essay: "La crépuscule du sens commun.")

Les Points sur les I. In *Les Oeuvres Libres*. Paris, 1958. Vol. 208.

Théâtre et religion. Lyon: Vitte, 1959.

L'Heure théâtrale: de Giraudoux à Jean-Paul Sartre. Paris: Plon, 1959.

Regards sur le théâtre de Claudel. Paris: Beauchesne, 1964.

Un juste. In *Paix sur la terre*. Paris: Aubier, 1965.

Le Secret est dans les îles: Le Dard, l'Emissaire, La Fin des temps. Paris: Plon, 1957.

Cinq pièces majeures: Un Homme de Dieu, Le Monde cassé, Le Chemin de Crête, La Soif, Le Signe de la Croix. Paris: Plon, 1973.

Percées vers un ailleurs: L'Iconoclaste, L'Horizon. (With essay: "L'Audace en métaphysique." Paris: Fayard, 1973.)